C000185439

FROM DAY TO DAY

WITH
D L MOODY

AMBASSADOR

BELFAST, NORTHERN IRELAND
GREENVILLE, USA

FROM DAY TO DAY

WITH
D L MOODY

Selected by
Emma Moody Fitt

AMBASSADOR

BELFAST, NORTHERN IRELAND
GREENVILLE, USA

From Day to Day with D L Moody

ISBN 1   84030 107 4

Ambassador Publications
a division of
Ambassador Productions Ltd.
Providence House
Ardenlee Street,
Belfast,
BT6 8QJ
Northern Ireland
www.ambassador-productions.com

Emerald House
427 Wade Hampton Blvd.
Greenville
SC 29609, USA
www.emeraldhouse.com

MR. MOODY'S FAVORITE TEXTS.

Behold, God is my salvation; I will trust and not be afraid; for the Lord Jehovah is my strength and my song; he also is become my salvation.—Isaiah 12:2.

The Lord God will help me, therefore shall I not be confounded, therefore have I set my face like a flint, and I know I shall not be ashamed.—Isaiah 50:7.

January 1st.

*Peace I leave with you, My peace I give unto you:
not as the world giveth, give I unto you. Let not your
heart be troubled, neither let it be afraid.*—John
xiv. 27.

DID you ever think that when Christ was
dying on the cross, He made a will?
Perhaps you have thought that no one ever remembered you in a will. If you are in the
kingdom, Christ remembered you in His. He
willed His body to Joseph of Arimathea, He
willed His mother to John, the son of Zebedee,
and He willed His spirit back to His Father.
But to His disciples He said,

" My peace, I leave that with you; that is
My legacy. My joy, I give that to you."

" My joy," think of it! " My peace "—not
our peace, but *His* peace!

They say a man can't make a will now that
lawyers can't break, and drive a four-in-hand
right straight through it. I will challenge them
to break Christ's will; let them try it. No
judge or jury can set that aside. Christ rose to
execute His own will. If He had left us a lot
of gold, thieves would have stolen it in the first
century; but He left His peace and His joy for
every true believer, and no power on earth can
take it from him who trusts.

January 2d.

For all the promises of God in Him are yea, and in Him Amen, unto the glory of God by us.—2 Corinthians i. 20.

IS there any reason why you should not have faith in God? Has God ever broken His Word? I defy any infidel to come forward and put his finger on any promise God has ever made to man that He has not kept.

I can show how for six thousand years the devil has lied, and how he has broken every promise he has made. What a lie he told Adam and Eve! Yet I can find a thousand men that will believe the devil's lies sooner than I can find one man that will believe God's truth.

January 3d.

By this shall all men know that ye are My disciples, if ye have love one to another.—John xiii. 35.

HOW are you going to tell whether you are a Christian or not? Not by the fact that you are a Catholic or a Protestant, not that you subscribe to some creed that man has drawn up. We must have something better than that. What did Christ say? " By this shall all men know that ye are My disciples, if ye have love one to another."

When I was first converted. I used to wish

that every Christian would wear a badge, because I would like to know them; my heart went out toward the household of faith. But I have got over that. Every hypocrite would have a badge inside of thirty days, if Christianity should become popular. No badge outside; but God gives us a badge in the heart. The man that hasn't any love in his creed may let it go to the winds; I don't want it. "By this shall all men know that ye are My disciples, if ye have love one to another." Love is the fruit of the Spirit. "If any man have not the Spirit of Christ, he is none of His."

JANUARY 4th.

For here have we no continuing city, but we seek one to come.—Hebrews xiii. 14.

SURELY it is not wrong for us to think and talk about heaven. I like to locate it, and find out all I can about it. I expect to live there through all eternity. If I were going to dwell in any place in this country, if I were going to make it my home, I would inquire about its climate, about the neighbors I would have, about everything, in fact, that I could learn concerning it. If soon you were going to emigrate, that is the way you would feel. Well, we are all going to emigrate in a very little while. We are going to spend eternity in another world, a grand and glorious world where God reigns. Is it not natural that we should look and listen and try to find out who is already there, and what is the route to take?

January 5th.

He came unto His own, and His own received Him not, but as many as received Him, to them gave He power to become the sons of God.—John i. 11, 12.

HIM—mark you—not a dogma, not a creed, not a myth, but A PERSON!

January 6th.

Heaven and earth shall pass away, but My Word shall not pass away.—Matthew xxiv. 35.

NOTICE how that statement has been fulfilled. There was no short-hand reporter following Jesus around taking down His words; there were no papers to print His sermons, and they wouldn't have printed them if there had been any daily papers. The leaders of the people were against Him.

I can see one of your modern freethinkers standing near Christ, and he hears Him say: "Heaven and earth shall pass away, but My Words shall not pass away." I see the scornful look on his face as he says: "Hear that Jewish peasant talk! Did you ever hear such conceit, such madness ? He says heaven and earth shall pass away, but His Word shall not pass away."

My friend, I want to ask you this question—has it passed away? Do you know that the sun has shone on more Bibles to-day than ever before in the history of the world? There have been more Bibles printed in the last ten years than in the first eighteen hundred years. They tried in the dark ages to burn it, to chain it, and keep it from the nations, but God has preserved it, and sent it to the ends of the earth.

JANUARY 7th.

And it shall come to pass, that before they call, I will answer ; and while they are yet speaking, I will hear.—Isaiah lxv. 24.

WE talk about heaven being so far away. It is within speaking distance to those who belong there.

JANUARY 8th.

But Abraham said, Son, remember that thou in thy lifetime receivedst thy good things, and likewise Lazarus evil things : but now he is comforted, and thou art tormented.—Luke xvi. 25.

I BELIEVE that when God touches the secret spring of memory, every one of our sins will come back, if they have not been blotted out by the blood of the Lord Jesus Christ, and they will haunt us as eternal ages roll on.

We talk about forgetting, but we cannot forget if God says " Remember ! " We talk about the recording angel keeping the record of our life. I have an idea that when we get to heaven, or into eternity, we will find that the recording angel has been ourselves. God will make every one of us keep our own record; memory will keep the record; and when God shall say, " Son, remember," it will all flash across our mind. It won't be God who will condemn us. We shall condemn ourselves, and we shall stand before God speechless.

JANUARY 9th.

And the Lord God said unto the woman, What is this that thou hast done? And the woman said, The serpent beguiled me, and I did eat.—Genesis iii. 13.

WHAT had she done? She had disobeyed God. She had turned from the fountain of life to the fountain of death, and had drunk from that fountain. She had introduced sin into the world.

God let her live long enough on the face of the earth to see what she had done. The first child that was born after the fall was a murderer. Bear in mind that sin leaped into this world full grown. The woman had gained for herself a fallen nature, and she transmitted it to her posterity. She lived nearly a thousand years if she

lived as long as Adam, and had a chance to see
something of the untold woe and misery she
had introduced into this world.

JANUARY 10th.

*If I regard iniquity in my heart, the Lord will not
hear me.*—Psalm lxvi. 18.

I SOMETIMES tremble when I hear people
quote promises, and say that God is bound to
fulfill those promises to them, when all the time
there is some sin in their lives they are not willing to give up. It is well for us to search our
hearts, and find out why it is that our prayers
are not answered.

JANUARY 11th.

*He answered and said, A man that is called Jesus
made clay, and anointed mine eyes, and said unto me, Go
to the pool of Siloam, and wash: and I went and
washed, and I received sight.*—John ix. 11.

HE told a straightforward story, just what the
Lord had done for him. That is all.
That is what a witness ought to do—tell what
he knows, not what he does not know. He
did not try to make a long speech. It is not
the most flippant and fluent witness who has
the most influence with a jury.

This man's testimony is what I call " experience." One of the greatest hindrances to
the progress of the gospel to-day is that the

narration of the experience of the Church is not encouraged. There are a great many men and women who come into the Church, and we never hear anything of the Lord's dealings with them. If we did, it would be a great help to others. It would stimulate faith and encourage the more feeble of the flock. The apostle Paul's experience has been recorded three times. I have no doubt that he told it everywhere he went: how God had met him; how God had opened his eyes and his heart; and how God had blessed him.

Depend upon it, experience has its place; the great mistake that is made now is in the other extreme. In some places and at some periods there has been too much of it—it has been all experience; and now we have let the pendulum swing too far the other way.

JANUARY 12th.

He answered and said, Lo, I see four men loose, walking in the midst of the fire, and they have no hurt; and the form of the fourth is like the Son of God.—Daniel iii. 25.

IT was doubtless the Son of God. That Great Shepherd of the sheep saw three of His true servants in peril, and He came from His Father's presence and His Father's bosom to be with them in it. He had been watching that terrible attempt to burn the faithful. His tender pitying

eye saw that they were condemned to death because of their loyalty to Him. With one great
leap He sprang from the Father's presence, from
His palace in glory, right down into the fiery
furnace, and was by their side before the heat
of the fire could come near unto them. Jesus
was with His servants as the flames wreathed
around them, and not a hair of their heads was
singed. They were not scorched; not even
the smell of fire was upon them. I can almost
fancy I hear them chanting:

"When thou passest through the waters I
will be with thee; and through the rivers, they
shall not overflow thee; *when thou walkest
through the fire, thou shalt not be burned; neither
shall the flame kindle upon thee.*"

JANUARY 13th.

*The Son of Man is come to seek and to save that
which was lost.*—Luke xix. 10.

TO me this is one of the sweetest verses in the
whole Bible. In this one short sentence
we are told what Christ came into this world
for. He came for a purpose, He came to do a
work. He came not to condemn the world, but
that the world through Him might be saved.

January 14th.

And one cried unto another, and said: Holy, holy, holy is the Lord of hosts: the whole earth is full of His glory.—Isaiah vi. 3.

WHEN we see the holiness of God, we shall adore and magnify Him. Moses learned this lesson. God told him to take his shoes from off his feet, for the place whereon he stood was holy ground. When we hear men trying to make out that they are holy, and speaking about their holiness, they make light of the holiness of God. It is His holiness that we need to think and speak about; when we do that, we shall be prostrate in the dust.

January 15th.

And thou, Capernaum, which art exalted unto heaven, shalt be brought down to hell: for if the mighty works, which have been done in thee, had been done in Sodom, it would have remained until this day. —Matthew xi. 23.

A MAN said to me some time ago: "Don't you think David fell as low as Saul?"

Yes, he fell lower, because God had lifted him up higher. The difference is that when Saul fell there was no sign of repentance, but when David fell, a wail went up from his broken heart, there was true repentance.

JANUARY 16th.

*So they read in the book in the law of God distinctly,
and gave the sense, and caused them to understand the
reading.*—Nehemiah viii. 8.

WE must study the Bible thoroughly, and
hunt it through, as it were, for some
great truth.

If a friend were to see me searching about
a building, and were to come up and say,
"Moody, what are you looking for? have you
lost something?" and I answered, "No, I
haven't lost anything; I'm not looking for anything in particular," I fancy he would just let me
go on by myself, and think me very foolish.
But if I were to say, "Yes, I have lost a dollar," why, I might expect him to help me to
find it.

Read the Bible as if you were seeking for
something of value. It is a good deal better to
take a single chapter, and spend a month on it,
than to read the Bible at random for a month.

JANUARY 17th.

*Who shall separate us from the love of Christ?
shall tribulation, or distress, or persecution, or famine,
or nakedness, or peril, or sword?*—Romans viii. 35.

NOW, who is going to do it? Devils?
men? angels? Paul throws down a
challenge. He challenges heaven, and earth,
and angels, and men, and principalities and

powers; and not only that, but all things past, present and to come; all creatures, internal or external; all states, death or life, height or preferment, depth or dungeon, prison or stripes.

Nothing shall separate me from the love of Christ. Let my enemies come collectively or singly, I don't care. Let them come one and all. I have no foes that can overcome me. Why? Because God has justified me. I do not dread death. Why? Because Christ has tasted death for me. I dread no judgment. Why? That is past. I dread no separation, and I anticipate no failure.

JANUARY 18th.

And they that be wise shall shine as the brightness of the firmament; and they that turn many to righteousness as the stars for ever and ever.—Daniel xii. 3.

HOW empty and short-lived are the glory and the pride of this world! If we are wise, we will live for God and eternity; we will get outside of ourselves, and will care nothing for the honor and glory of this world. In Proverbs we read: "He that winneth souls is wise." If any man, woman, or child by a godly life and example can win one soul to God, their life will not have been a failure. They will have outshone all the mighty men of their day, because they will have set a stream in motion that will flow on and on forever and ever.

JANUARY 19th.

I the Lord search the heart, I try the reins, even to give every man according to his ways, and according to the fruit of his doings.—Jeremiah xvii. 10.

WHEN I was going through the land of Goshen in Egypt a few years ago, as I came near the city of Alexandria I saw one of the strangest sights I had ever seen. The heavens were lit up with a new kind of light, and there seemed to be flash after flash; I couldn't understand it. I found later that the Khedive had died, and that a new Khedive was coming into power. England had sent over some war vessels, and the moment darkness came on they had turned their searchlights upon the city. It was almost as light as noonday. Every street was lit up, and I do not suppose that ten men could have met in any part of Alexandria without being discovered by that searchlight.

May God turn His searchlight upon us, and see if there be any evil way in us!

JANUARY 20th.

And Enoch walked with God: and he was not : for God took him.—Genesis v. 24.

By faith Enoch was translated that he should not see death ; and was not found, because God had translated him : for before his translation he had this testimony, that he pleased God.—Hebrews xi. 5.

A GREAT deal is being said about holiness. Every true child of God desires to be holy, as His Father in heaven is holy. And holiness

is walking with God. Enoch had only one object. How simple life becomes when we have
only one object to seek, one purpose to fulfill—
to walk with God, to please God! It has been
said that the utmost many Christians get to is
that they are pardoned criminals. How short
they fall of the joy and blessedness of walking
with God!

JANUARY 21st.

*Thine own wickedness shall correct thee, and thy
backslidings shall reprove thee : know therefore and see
that it is an evil thing and bitter, that thou hast forsaken the Lord thy God, and that My fear is not in
thee, saith the Lord God of hosts.*—Jeremiah ii. 19.

I HAVE travelled a good deal, but I never found
a happy backslider in my life. I never knew
a man who was really born of God that ever
could find the world satisfy him afterward. Do
you think the prodigal son was satisfied in that
foreign country? Ask the prodigals to-day if
they are truly happy. You know they are not.
"There is no peace, saith my God, to the
wicked."

JANUARY 22d.

*Verily I say unto you, Except ye be converted, and
become as little children, ye shall not enter into the
kingdom of heaven.*—Matthew xviii. 3.

I T is a master-piece of the devil to make us believe that children cannot understand religion. Would Christ have made a child the

standard of faith if He had known that it was not capable of understanding His words ? It is far easier for children to love and trust than for grown-up persons, and so we should set Christ before them as the supreme object of their choice.

JANUARY 23d.

If thou shalt confess with thy mouth the Lord Jesus, and shalt believe in thine heart that God hath raised Him from the dead, thou shalt be saved.—Romans x. 9.

I DO not know of any more important truth to bring before an unconverted person than the answer to the question—" What must I do to be saved ? "—because that is the beginning of everything with regard to the divine life. A man must know he is saved before there is any peace, or joy, or comfort. The answer is, " Believe on the Lord Jesus Christ, and thou shalt be saved."

The question that comes right after that from almost every one is, " What is it to believe ? " I believe that Jesus Christ is the Son of God ; I believe that He came into the world to save sinners. Well, so do the devils. The devils not only believe, but they tremble. I can believe intellectually that Jesus Christ is able and willing to save, and yet be as far from the kingdom of God as any man who never heard about Jesus Christ. To be saved I must believe in my heart, and trust in His atoning work.

JANUARY 24th.

And the ransomed of the Lord shall return, and come to Zion with songs and everlasting joy upon their heads: they shall obtain joy and gladness, and sorrow and sighing shall flee away.—Isaiah xxxv. 10.

JOSEPH PARKER of London uttered something that I thought was splendid in regard to the thirty-fifth of Isaiah, where it says: "Sorrow and sighing shall flee away." Take up an old dictionary, he said, and once in a while you will come across a word marked "obsolete." The time is coming, he said, when those two words, "sorrow" and "sighing" shall be obsolete. Sighing and sorrow shall flee away, to be no more. Thank God for the outlook!

JANUARY 25th.

O Lord, open Thou my lips; and my mouth shall show forth Thy praise!—Psalm li. 15.

IT is a very sad thing that so many of God's children are dumb; yet it is true. Parents would think it a great calamity to have their children born dumb; they would mourn over it, and weep, and well they might; but did you ever think of the many dumb children God has? The churches are full of them. They can talk about politics, art, and science; they can speak well enough and fast enough about the fashions of the day; but they have no voice for the Son of God.

Dear friend, if Christ is your Saviour, confess Him. Every follower of Jesus should bear testimony for Him. How many opportunities each one has in society and in business to speak a word for Him! How many opportunities occur daily wherein every Christian might be "instant in season and out of season" in pleading for Jesus! In so doing we receive blessing for ourselves, and also become a means of blessing to others.

JANUARY 26th.

Endeavoring to keep the unity of the Spirit in the bond of peace.—Ephesians iv. 3.

ONE of the saddest things in the present day is the division in God's church. You notice that when the power of God came upon the early church, it was when they were " all of one accord." I believe the blessing of Pentecost never would have been given but for that spirit of unity. If they had been divided and quarrelling among themselves, do you think the Holy Ghost would have come, and those thousands been converted?

I have noticed in our work, that if we have gone to a town where three churches were united in it, we have had greater blessing than if only one church was in sympathy. And if there have been twelve churches united, the blessing has multiplied fourfold; it has always been in proportion to the spirit of unity that has been manifested. Where there are bickerings and divisions, and where the spirit of unity is absent, there is very little blessing and praise.

JANUARY 27th.

Search me, O God, and know my heart: try me, and know my thoughts: and see if there be any wicked way in me, and lead me in the way everlasting.—Psalm cxxxix. 23, 24.

IF we should all honestly make this prayer once every day, there would be a good deal of change in our lives. " *Search* ME "—not my neighbor. It is so easy to pray for other people, but so hard to get home to ourselves. I am afraid that we who are busy in the Lord's work, are especially in danger of neglecting our own vineyard. In this Psalm, David got home to himself.

There is a difference between God searching me and my searching myself. I may search my heart, and pronounce it all right, but when God searches me as with a lighted candle, a good many things will come to light that perhaps I knew nothing about.

JANUARY 28th.

Where your treasure is, there will your heart be also.—Matthew vi. 21.

IT does not take long to tell where a man's treasure is. In fifteen minutes' conversation with most men you can tell whether their treasures are on earth or in heaven. Talk to a patriot about his country, and you will see his eye light up; you will find he has his heart there. Talk to business men, and tell them where they can make a thousand dollars, and see their interest; their hearts are there. Talk to people who are living just for fashion, of its affairs, and you will see their eyes kindle, they are interested at once; their hearts are there. Talk to a politician about politics, and you see how suddenly he becomes interested. And talk to a child of God, who is really laying up treasures in heaven, about heaven and about his future home, and he responds at once, there are chords in his heart that vibrate at the thought of heaven and home.

JANUARY 29th.

Godliness with contentment is great gain.—1 Timothy vi. 6.

WOULD to God we might all be able to say with Paul—"I have coveted no man's silver, or gold, or apparel." The Lord had made him partaker of His grace, and he was soon to be a partaker of His glory, and earthly things looked very small. "Godliness with contentment is great gain," he wrote to Timothy; "having food and raiment, therewith let us be content." Observe that he puts godliness first. No worldly gain can satisfy the human heart. Roll the whole world in and still there would be room.

JANUARY 30th.

And he said, I heard Thy voice in the garden, and I was afraid, because I was naked; and I hid myself.—Genesis iii. 10.

MOST of us live away from home. We are hiding as Adam did in the bushes of Eden. There was a time when God's voice thrilled Adam's soul with joy and gladness, and he thrilled God's heart with joy. They lived in sweet fellowship with each other. God had lifted Adam to the very gates of heaven, had made him lord over all creation. I haven't a doubt that He had plans to raise Adam still higher—higher than the angels, higher than seraphim and cherubim, higher than Gabriel, who stands in the presence of Jehovah, and Michael, the archangel. But the man turned and became a traitor to Him who wanted to bless him.

JANUARY 31st.

As many as received Him, to them gave He power to become the sons of God, even to them that believe on His name.—John i. 12.

YES, sons of God! Power to overcome the world, the flesh, and the devil; power to crucify every besetting sin, passion, lust; power to shout in triumph over every trouble and temptation of life, " I can do all things through Christ which strengtheneth me ! "

FEBRUARY 1st.

Yea, though I walk through the valley of the shadow of death, I will fear no evil: for Thou art with me; Thy rod and Thy staff they comfort me.—Psalm xxiii. 4.

MUST not there be light where there is shadow? Can you get a shadow without light? If you doubt it, go down into the cellar to-night without a light, and find your shadow if you can. All that death can do to a true believer is to throw a shadow across his path. Shadows never hurt any one. You can walk right through them as you can through fog. There is nothing to fear.

I pity down deep in my heart any man or woman that lives under the bondage of death! If you are under it, may God bring you out to-day! May you come right out into the liberty of the blessed gospel of the Son of God!

FEBRUARY 2d.

If any man be in Christ, he is a new creature: old things are passed away; behold, all things are become new.—2 Corinthians v. 17.

ALL the infidels in the world could not convince me that I have not a different spirit than I had before I became a Christian. "That which is born of the flesh is flesh, and that which is born of the Spirit is spirit," and a man can soon tell whether he is born of the Spirit by the change in his life. The Spirit of Christ is a Spirit of love, joy, peace, humility and meekness, and we can soon find out whether we have been born of that Spirit or not; we are not to be left in uncertainty.

FEBRUARY 3d.

The promise is unto you, and to your children, and to all that are afar off, even as many as the Lord our God shall call.—Acts ii. 39.

IT is not only our privilege to have our names written in heaven, but also those of the children whom God has given us; and our hearts ought to go right out for them. The promise is not only to us, but to our children. Many a father's and many a mother's heart is burdened with anxiety for the salvation of their children. If your own name is there, let your next aim in life be to get your children's there also.

FEBRUARY 4th.

From within, out of the heart of men, proceed evil thoughts, adulteries, fornications, murders, thefts, covetousness, wickedness, deceit, lasciviousness, an evil eye, blasphemy, pride, foolishness.—Mark vii. 21, 22.

IF a man should advertise that he could take a correct photograph of people's hearts, do you believe he would find any customers? There is not a man among us whom you could hire to have his photograph taken, if you could photograph the real man. We go to have our faces taken, and carefully arrange our toilet, and if the artist flatters us, we say, " Oh, yes, that's a first-rate likeness," and we pass it around among our friends. But let the real man be brought out, the photograph of the heart, and see if we will pass that around among our neighbors! Why, we would not want our own wives to see it! We would be frightened even to look at it ourselves.

FEBRUARY 5th.

(Mr. D. L. Moody's birthday.)

He asked life of Thee, and Thou gavest it him, even length of days for ever and ever.—Psalm xxi. 4.

I WAS down in Texas some time ago, and happened to pick up a newspaper, and there they called me " Old Moody." Honestly, I never got such a shock from any paper in my life before! I never had been called old before. I went to my hotel, and looked in the looking-glass. I cannot conceive of getting old. I have a life that is never going to end. Death may change my position but not my condition, not my standing with Jesus Christ. Death is not going to separate us.

Old! I wish you all felt as young as I do here to-night. Why, I am only sixty-two years old! If you meet me ten million years hence, then I will be young. Read that ninety

first Psalm, " With long life will I satisfy him."
That doesn't mean seventy years. Would that
satisfy you? Did you ever see a man or woman
of seventy satisfied? Don't they want to live
longer? You know that seventy wouldn't
satisfy you. Would eighty? would ninety?
would one hundred? If Adam had lived to be
a million years old, and then had to die, he
wouldn't be satisfied. " With long life will I
satisfy him "—life without end! Don't call me
old. I am only sixty-two. I have only begun
to live.

FEBRUARY 6th.

*Now I, Nebuchadnezzar, praise and extol and honor
the King of heaven, all whose works are truth, and
His ways judgment: and those that walk in pride He is
able to abase.*—Daniel iv. 37.

WHEN you find that a man has got to praising God it is a good sign. Nebuchadnezzar's earlier edict said much about other
people's duty toward the God of the Hebrews,
but nothing about what the king himself should
do. Oh, let us get to personal love, personal
praise! That is what is wanted in the church
in the present day.

Nebuchadnezzar passes from the stage: this
is the last record we have of him. But we may
surely hope that his was a " repentance to salvation not to be repented of." If so, we may

well believe that to-day Nebuchadnezzar the king and Daniel the captive are walking the crystal pavement of heaven arm-in-arm together; and, it may be, talking over the old times in Babylon.

FEBRUARY 7th.

Ye are our epistle written in our hearts, known and read of all men.—2 Corinthians iii. 2.

I REMEMBER reading of a blind man who was found sitting at the corner of a street in a great city with a lantern beside him. Some one went up to him and asked what he had the lantern there for, seeing that he was blind, and the light was the same to him as the darkness. The blind man replied :

"I have it so that no one may stumble over me."

Where one man reads the Bible, a hundred read you and me. That is what Paul meant when he said we were to be living epistles of Christ, known and read of all men. I would not give much for all that can be done by sermons, if we do not preach Christ by our lives. If we do not commend the gospel to people by our holy walk and conversation, we shall not win them to Christ.

February 8th.

Though I speak with the tongues of men and of angels, and have not love, I am become as sounding brass, or a tinkling cymbal. And though I have the gift of prophecy, and understand all mysteries, and all knowledge; and though I have all faith, so that I could remove mountains, and have not love, I am nothing.— 1 Corinthians xiii. 1, 2.

A MAN may have wonderful knowledge, may be able to unravel the mysteries of the Bible, and yet be as cold as an icicle. He may glisten like the snow in the sun. Sometimes you have wondered why it was that certain ministers who have had such wonderful magnetism, who have such a marvellous command of language, and who preach with such mental strength, haven't had more conversions. I believe, if the truth was known, you would find no divine love back of their words, no pure love in their sermons.

February 9th.

*Thou wilt keep him in perfect peace, whose mind is stayed on thee: because he trusteth in Thee. Trust ye in the Lord for ever: for in the Lord Jehovah is everlasting strength.—*Isaiah xxvi. 3, 4.

A S long as our mind is stayed on our dear selves, we will never have peace. Some people think more of themselves than of all the rest of the world. It is self in the morning, self at noon, and self at night. It is self when they wake up, and self when they go to bed. They are all the time looking at themselves and thinking about themselves, instead of " looking unto Jesus." Faith is an outward look. Faith does not look within; it looks without. It is not what I think, or what I feel, or what I have done, but it is what Jesus Christ is and has done, that is the important thing for us to dwell upon.

FEBRUARY 10th.

And the Lord spake unto Moses, saying, Speak unto Aaron and unto his sons, saying, On this wise ye shall bless the children of Israel, saying unto them : The Lord bless thee and keep thee : the Lord make His face shine upon thee, and be gracious unto thee : the Lord lift up His countenance upon thee, and give thee peace.— Numbers vi. 22.

I THINK these are about as sweet verses as we find in the Old Testament. I marked them years ago in my Bible, and many times I have turned to this chapter and read them. They remind us of the loving words of Jesus to His troubled disciples, " It is I : be not afraid." The Jewish salutation used to be, as a man went into a house, " Peace be upon this house," and as he left the house the host would say, " Go in peace."

FEBRUARY 11th.

*The secret things belong unto the Lord our God:
but those things which are revealed belong unto us and
to our children for ever, that we may do all the words
of this law.*—Deuteronomy xxix. 29.

THERE are many things which were dark
and mysterious to me five years ago, on
which I have since had a flood of light; and I
expect to be finding out something fresh about
God throughout eternity.

I make a point of not discussing disputed
passages of Scripture. An old divine has said
that some people, if they want to eat fish, com-
mence by picking the bones. I leave such
things till I have light on them. I am not
bound to explain what I do not comprehend.
" The secret things belong unto the Lord our
God: but those things which are revealed belong unto us, and to our children forever "; and
these I take, and eat, and feed upon, in order
to get spiritual strength.

FEBRUARY 12th.

*And at midnight Paul and Silas prayed, and sang
praises unto God: and the prisoners heard them.*—
Acts xvi. 25.

AN old gentleman got up once in a meeting
and said he had lived nearly all his life on
Grumble street, but not long ago he had moved

over on Thanksgiving street. His face showed
it. Paul and Silas in jail at Philippi, when they
had received stripes on the back and had their
feet in the stocks, still sang praises to God. If
some of us were in jail, with our feet in the
stocks, I don't think we would sing much. We
want a cheerful Christianity.

FEBRUARY 13th.

*Therefore let all the house of Israel know assuredly,
that God hath made that same Jesus, whom ye have
crucified, both Lord and Christ. Now when they heard
this, they were pricked in their heart, and said unto
Peter and to the rest of the apostles, Men and brethren, what shall we do? Then Peter said unto them,
Repent, and be baptized every one of you in the name of
Jesus Christ for the remission of sins, and ye shall receive the gift of the Holy Ghost.—Acts ii. 36–38.*

ONE thing I have noticed, that some conversions don't amount to anything; that if a
man professes to be converted without conviction of sin, he is one of those stony-ground
hearers who don't bring forth much fruit. The
first little wave of persecution, the first breath
of opposition, and the man is back in the world
again. Let us pray that God may carry on a
deep and thorough work, that men may be convicted of sin so that they cannot rest in unbelief. Pray that this conviction and confession
may begin in our own church. I would a great
deal rather see a hundred men thoroughly con-

verted, truly born of God, than to see a thousand professed conversions where the Spirit of God has not convicted of sin.

For ye know the grace of our Lord Jesus Christ, that, though He was rich, yet for our sakes He became poor, that ye through His poverty might be rich.—2 Corinthians viii. 9.

MEN talk about grace, but, as a rule, they know very little about it. Let a business man go to a banker's to borrow a few hundred dollars for sixty or ninety days; if he is well able to pay, the banker will perhaps lend him the money if he can get another responsible man to sign the note with him. They give what they call "three days' grace" after the sixty or ninety days have expired; but they will make the borrower pay interest on the money during these three days, and if he does not return principal and interest at the appointed time, they will sell his goods; they will perhaps turn him out of his house, and take the last piece of furniture in his possession.

That is not grace at all, but that fairly illustrates man's idea of it. Grace not only frees from payment of the interest, but of the principal also. The grace of God frees us from the penalty of our sin without any payment on our part. Christ has paid the debt, and all we have to do is to believe on Him for our salvation.

FEBRUARY 15th.

For ye have not received the spirit of bondage again to fear; but ye have received the spirit of adoption, whereby Ye cry, Abba, Father.—Romans viii. 15.

I WANT to say very emphatically that I have no sympathy with the doctrine of universal brotherhood, and universal fatherhood; I don't believe one word of it. If a man lives in the flesh and serves the flesh, he is a child of the devil. That is pretty strong language, but it is what Christ said. It brought down a hornet's nest on His head, and helped to hasten Him to the cross, but nevertheless it is true. Show me a man that will lie and steal and get drunk and ruin a woman,—do you tell me he is my brother? Not a bit of it. He must be born into the household of faith before he becomes my brother in Christ. He is an alien, he is a stranger to the grace of God, he is an enemy to God, he is not a friend. Before a man can cry, " Abba, Father, " he must be born from above, born of the Spirit.

FEBRUARY 16th.

I am the resurrection and the life : he that believeth in Me, though he were dead, yet shall he live.
—John xi. 25.

WHEN a young man, I was called upon suddenly, in Chicago, to preach a funeral sermon. A good many Chicago business men were to be there, and I said to myself,

"Now, it will be a good chance for me to preach the gospel to those men, and I will get one of Christ's funeral sermons."

I hunted all through the four Gospels trying to find one of Christ's funeral sermons, but I couldn't find any. I found He broke up every funeral He ever attended! He never preached a funeral sermon in the world. Death couldn't exist where He was. When the dead heard His voice they sprang to life.

FEBRUARY 17th.

The heart is deceitful above all things, and desperately wicked: who can know it?—Jeremiah xvii. 9.

NOBODY knows what is in the human heart but Christ. We do not know our own hearts; none of us have any idea how bad they are. Some bitter things have been written against me, but I know a good many more things about myself that are bad than any other man. There is nothing good in the old Adam nature. We have got a heart in rebellion against God by nature, and we do not even love God unless we are born of the Spirit.

This is a truth that men do not at all like, but I have noticed that the medicine that we do not like is often the medicine that will do us good. If we do not think we are as bad as the description, we must just take a closer look at ourselves.

February 18th.

Being born again, not of corruptible seed, but of incorruptible, by the word of God, which liveth and abideth for ever.—1 Peter i. 23.

WE hear nowadays so much about " culture." Culture's all right when you have something to cultivate. If I should plant a watch, I shouldn't get any little watches, would I? Why? Because the seed of life is not there. But let me plant some peas or potatoes, and I will get a crop.

Don't let any man or woman rest short of being born of the Spirit of God. Don't cultivate a dead and corrupt thing, first make sure that you have that divine nature, then cultivate it.

February 19th.

Behold, I set before you this day a blessing and a curse; a blessing, if ye obey the commandments of the Lord your God, which I command you this day: and a curse, if ye will not obey the commandments of the Lord your God, but turn aside out of the way which I command you this day, to go after other gods, which ye have not known.—Deuteronomy xi. 26–28.

TAKE the two Sauls. They lived about one thousand years apart. One started out well and ended poorly, and the other started out poorly and ended well.

The first Saul got a kingdom and a crown;

he had a lovely family, (no father ever had a better son than Saul had in Jonathan); he had the friendship of Samuel, the best prophet there was on the face of the earth; and yet he lost the friendship of Samuel, lost his crown, his kingdom and his life, all through an act of disobedience.

Now take the Saul of the New Testament. When God called him he was obedient to the heavenly vision, and he was given a heavenly kingdom.

One act of obedience, one act of disobedience. The act of obedience gained all, and the act of disobedience lost everything. I believe the wretchedness and misery and woe in this country to-day comes from disobedience to God. If they won't obey God as a nation, let us begin individually. Let us make up our minds that we will do it, cost us what it will; and we will have peace and joy.

FEBRUARY 20th.

He that turneth away his ear from hearing the law, even his prayer shall be abomination.—Proverbs xxviii. 9.

THINK of that! It may shock some of us to think that our prayers are an abomination to God, yet if any are living in known sin, this is what God's Word says about them. If we are not willing to turn from sin and obey

God's law, we have no right to expect that He will answer our prayers. Unconfessed sin is unforgiven sin, and unforgiven sin is the darkest, foulest thing on this sin-cursed earth. You cannot find a case in the Bible where a man has been honest in dealing with sin, but God has been honest with him and blessed him. The prayer of the humble and the contrite heart is a delight to God. There is no sound that goes up from this sin-cursed earth so sweet to His ear as the prayer of the man who is walking uprightly.

FEBRUARY 21st.

In the last day, that great day of the feast, Jesus stood and cried, saying, If any man thirst, let him come unto Me, and drink. He that believeth on Me, as the Scripture hath said, out of his belly shall flow rivers of living water.—John vii. 37, 38.

WHEN a boy upon a farm in New England, we had a well, and I used to have to pump the water from that well upon wash-day, and to water the cattle; and many a time I had to pump and pump and pump until my arm got tired. But they have a better way now. They don't dig down a few feet and brick up the hole and put the pump in, but they go down through the clay and the sand and the rock, on down until they strike what they call a lower stream, and then it becomes an artesian well, which needs no labor, as the water rises spontaneously from the depths beneath.

I think God wants each of His children to be a sort of artesian well; not to keep pumping, but to flow right out. Why, haven't you seen ministers in the pulpit just pumping, pumping, pumping? I have, many a time, and I have had to do it, too. I know how it is. They stand in the pulpit and talk and talk and talk, and the people go to sleep, they can't arouse them. What is the trouble? Why, the living water is not there; they are just pumping when there is no water in the well.

FEBRUARY 22d.

But Thomas, one of the twelve, called Didymus, was not with them when Jesus came. The other disciples therefore said unto him, We have seen the Lord. But he said unto them, Except I shall see in His hands the print of the nails, and put my finger into the print of the nails, and thrust my hand into His side, I will not believe.—John xx. 24, 25.

I OFTEN think that Thomas was the most unhappy man in Jerusalem during the week that followed. It would have been far more reasonable for him to have believed those who saw Jesus, rather than to have doubted their word. But unbelief is the most unreasonable thing in the world.

FEBRUARY 23d.

I am persuaded, that neither death, nor life, nor angels, nor principalities, nor powers, nor things present, nor things to come, nor height, nor depth, nor any other creature, shall be able to separate us from the love of God, which is in Jesus Christ our Lord.—Romans viii. 38, 39.

THERE can be no true peace, there can be no true hope, there can be no true comfort, where there is uncertainty. I am not fit for God's service, I cannot go out and work for God, if I am in doubt about my own salvation.

FEBRUARY 24th.

And they took Lot, Abram's brother's son, who dwelt in Sodom, and his goods, and departed.—Genesis xiv. 12.

FOR awhile Lot did make money very fast in Sodom, and became a very successful man. If you had gone into Sodom a little while before destruction came, you would have found that Lot owned some of the best corner lots in town, and that Mrs. Lot moved in what they called the *bonton* society or upper ten; and you would have found that she was at the theatre two or three nights in the week. If they had progressive euchre, she could play as well as anybody; and her daughters could dance as well as any other Sodomites. We find Lot sitting in the gates, he is getting on amazingly well. He may have been one of the principal men in the city; Judge Lot, or the Honorable Mr. Lot of Sodom. They might have elected him Mayor of Sodom. He was getting on amazingly well; wonderfully prosperous.

But by and by there comes a war. If you go into Sodom, you must take Sodom's judgment when it comes; and it is bound to come. The battle turned against those five cities of the plain, and they took Lot and his wife and all that they had.

February 25th.

There was a certain creditor which had two debtors: the one owed five hundred pence, and the other fifty. And when they had nothing to pay, he frankly forgave them both.—Luke vii. 41, 42.

VERY few people think they are lost. You seldom meet a bankrupt sinner. Most of them think they can pay about seventy-five cents on the dollar; some ninety-nine per cent. —they just come short a little, and they think the Almighty will make it up somehow.

Don't let Satan make you think you are so good that you don't need the grace of God. We are a bad lot, all of us, with nothing to pay.

FEBRUARY 26th.

Remember the words of the Lord Jesus, how He said, It is more blessed to give than to receive.— Acts xx. 35.

WHAT makes the Dead Sea dead? Because it is all the time receiving, but never giving out anything. Why is it that many Christians are cold? Because they are all the time receiving, never giving out.

FEBRUARY 27th.

*My speech and my preaching was not with enticing words of man's wisdom, but in demonstration of the Spirit and of power.—*1 Corinthians. ii. 4.

MANY people think that we need new measures, that we need new churches, that we need new organs, and that we need new choirs, and all these new things. But what the Church of God needs to-day is the old power that the apostles had: if we have that in our churches, there will be new life. Then we will have new ministers—the same old ministers renewed with power, filled with the Spirit.

I remember when in Chicago many were toiling in the work, and it seemed as though the car of salvation didn't move on, when a minister began to cry out from the very depths of his heart, " Oh, God, put new ministers in every pulpit." The next Monday I heard two or

three men say, "We had a new minister last
Sunday—the same old minister, but he had got
new power." I firmly believe that is what we
want to-day all over the land. We want new
ministers in the pulpit and new people in the
pews. We want people quickened by the
Spirit of God.

February 28th.

*Strive to enter in at the strait gate: for many, I say
unto you, will seek to enter in, and shall not be able.—*
Luke xiii. 24.

WHO are we to strive with? Not with the
gate-keeper. The gate-keeper stands
with the gate wide open, and he says, " Come
in, come in!" All the striving is with the
flesh; it is with this old carnal nature of ours.

March 1st.

*Whom God hath raised up, having loosed the pains
of death: because it was not possible that He should be
holden of it.—*Acts ii. 24.

I CAN imagine when they laid our Lord in
Joseph's tomb one might have seen Death
sitting over that sepulcher, saying,

" I have Him; He is my victim. He said
He was the Resurrection and the Life. Now I
hold Him in my cold embrace. They thought
He was never going to die; but see Him now.
He has had to pay tribute to me."

Never! The glorious morning comes, the Son of man bursts asunder the hands of death, and rises, a conqueror, from the grave. "Because I live," He shouts, "ye shall live also." Yes, we *shall live also*—is it not good news?

MARCH 2d.

*If it be so, our God whom we serve is able to deliver us from the burning fiery furnace, and He will deliver us out of thine hand, O king. But if not, be it known unto thee, O king, that we will not serve thy gods, nor worship the golden image which thou hast set up.—*Daniel iii. 17, 18.

THOSE Hebrews spoke respectfully, but firmly. And mark, they did not absolutely say that God *would* deliver them from the burning fiery furnace; but they declared that He was *able* to deliver them. They had no doubt about His ability to do it. They believed that He could do it; but they did not hide from themselves the possibility of Nebuchadnezzar being allowed to carry out his threats. Still, that did not greatly move them. "But *if not*," —if in His inscrutable purposes He allows us to suffer,—"still our resolve is the same: we will not serve thy gods, nor worship the golden image which thou hast set up." They were not afraid to pass from the presence of the king of Babylon to the presence of the King of kings.

MARCH 3d.

He that overcometh shall inherit all things; and I will be his God, and he shall be My son.—Revelation xxi. 7.

I USED to have my Sabbath-school children sing—" I want to be an angel"; but I have not done so for years. We shall be above angels: we shall be sons of God. Just see what a kingdom we shall come into. We shall inherit all things! Do you ask me how much I am worth? I don't know. The Rothschilds cannot compute their wealth. They don't know how many millions they own. That is my condition—I haven't the slightest idea how much I am worth. God has no poor children. If we overcome we shall inherit all things.

MARCH 4th.

What doth it profit, my brethren, though a man say he hath faith, and have not works? can faith save him?—James ii. 14.

I BELIEVE in a faith that you can see; a living, working faith that prompts to action. Faith without works is like a man putting all his money into the foundation of a house; and works without faith is like building a house on sand without any foundation.

You often hear people say: " The root of the matter is in him." What would you say if I had a garden and nothing but roots in it?

MARCH 5th.

Howbeit, when He, the Spirit of Truth is come, He will guide you into all truth; for He shall not speak of Himself; but whatsoever He shall hear that shall He speak; and He will show you things to come.— John xvi. 13.

THERE is not a truth that we ought to know but the Spirit of God will guide us into it if we will let Him. If we will yield ourselves up to be directed by Him and let Him lead us, He will guide us into all truth. It would have saved us from a great many dark hours if we had only been willing to let the Spirit of God be our counsellor and guide.

Lot never would have gone to Sodom if he had been guided by the Spirit of God. David never would have fallen into sin and had all that trouble with his family if he had been guided by the Spirit of God.

There are many Lots and Davids nowadays. The churches are full of them. Men and women are in total darkness, because they have not been willing to be guided by the Spirit. " He shall guide you into all truth."

MARCH 6th.

It is good for me that I have been afflicted; that I might learn Thy statutes.—Psalm cxix. 71.

A DEAD level in a man's life would be his ruin ? If he had nothing but prosperity, he would be ruined. A man can stand adversity better than prosperity. I know a great many who have become very prosperous, but I know few such that haven't lost all their piety, that haven't lost sight of that city eternal in the heavens, whose builder and maker is God. Earthly things have drawn their heart's affections away from eternal things.

MARCH 7th.

Thine own wickedness shall correct thee, and thy backsliding shall reprove thee; know, therefore, and see, that it is an evil thing and bitter that thou hast forsaken the Lord thy God, and that My fear is not in thee, saith the Lord God of hosts.—Jeremiah xi. 19.

I DO not exaggerate when I say that I have seen hundreds of backsliders come back, and I have asked them if they had not found it an evil and a bitter thing to leave the Lord. You cannot find a real backslider, who has known the Lord, but will admit that it is an evil and a bitter thing to turn away from Him; and I do not know of any one verse more used to bring back wanderers than this very one.

Look at Lot. Did not he find it an evil and a bitter thing? He was twenty years in Sodom and never made a convert. Men would have told you that he was one of the most influential and worthy men in all Sodom. But alas! alas! he ruined his family. And it is a pitiful sight to see that old backslider going through the streets of Sodom at midnight, after he has warned his children, and they have turned a deaf ear to him.

MARCH 8th.

Rejoice, because your names are written in heaven.—Luke x. 20.

A SOLDIER, wounded during our civil war, lay dying in his cot. Suddenly the death-like stillness of the room was broken by the cry, " Here! Here!" which burst from the lips of the dying man. Friends rushed to the spot and asked what he wanted.

"Hark" he said, "they are calling the roll of heaven, and I am answering to my name."

In a few moments he whispered, " Here!" once more, and passed into the presence of the King.

MARCH 9th.

Ye also helping together by prayer for us, that for the gift bestowed upon us by the means of many persons thanks may be given by many on our behalf.—2 Corinthians i. 11.

YOU have heard the story of the child who was rescued from the fire that was raging in a house away up in the fourth story. The child came to the window, and as the flames were shooting up higher and higher cried out for help. A fireman started up the ladder. The wind swept the flames near him, and it was getting so hot that he wavered. Thousands looked on, and their hearts quaked at the thought of the child having to perish. Some one in the crowd cried: "Give him a cheer!" Cheer after cheer went up, and as the man heard he gathered fresh courage. Up he went into the midst of the smoke and the fire, and brought down the child in safety.

If you cannot go and rescue the perishing yourself, you can at least pray for those who do, and cheer them on. If you do, the Lord will bless the effort. Do not grumble and criticise; it takes neither heart nor brains to do that.

MARCH 10th.

Then said Jesus again unto them, I go my way, and ye shall seek Me, and shall die in your sins: whither I go, ye cannot come.—John viii. 21.

ONE sentence from the lips of the Son of God in regard to the future state has forever settled it in my mind. "Ye shall die in your sins; whither I go, ye cannot come." If a man has not given up his drunkenness, his profanity, his licentiousness, his covetousness, heaven would be hell to him. Heaven is a prepared place for prepared people. What would a man do in heaven who cannot bear to be in the society of the pure and holy down here?

MARCH 11th.

Moreover thou shalt provide out of all the people able men, such as fear God, men of truth, hating covetousness; and place such over them, to be rulers of thousands, and rulers of hundreds, rulers of fifties, and rulers of tens.—Exodus xviii. 21.

ISN'T it extraordinary that Jethro, the man of the desert, should have given this advice to Moses? How did he learn to beware of covetousness? We honor men to-day if they are wealthy and covetous. We elect them to office in church and state. We often say that they will make better treasurers because we know them to be covetous. But in God's sight a covetous man is as vile and black as any thief or drunkard. David said: "The wicked boasteth of his heart's desire, and blesseth the covetous, whom the Lord abhorreth." I am afraid that many who profess to have put away wickedness also speak well of the covetous.

MARCH 12th.

Beloved, now are we the sons of God, and it doth not yet appear what we shall be: but we know that, when He shall appear, we shall be like Him; for we shall see Him as He is.—1 John iii. 2.

THE reason why there are so many in the churches who will not go out and help others, is that they are not sure they have been saved themselves. If I thought I was dying myself, I would be in a poor condition to save any one else. Before I can pull any one else out of the water, I must have a firm footing on shore myself.

We can have this complete assurance if we will. It does not do to *feel* we are all right, we must *know* it. We must read our titles *clear* to mansions in the skies. The Apostle John says: "Beloved, *now* are we the sons of God." He does not say we are going to be.

March 13th.

Verily, verily, I say unto you, He that heareth My word, and believeth on Him that sent me, hath everlasting life, and shall not come into condemnation, but is passed from death unto life.—John v. 24.

IN my native village in New England it used to be customary, as a funeral procession left the church, for the bell to toll as many times as the deceased was years old. How anxiously I would count those strokes of the bell to see how long I might reckon on living! Sometimes there would be seventy or eighty tolls, and I would give a sigh of relief to think I had so many years to live. But at other times there would be only a few years tolled, and then a horror would seize me as I thought that I too might soon be claimed as a victim by that dread monster, Death. Death and judgment were a constant source of fear to me till I realized the fact that neither shall ever have any hold on a child of God.

March 14th.

For their rock is not as our Rock, even our enemies themselves being judges.—Deuteronomy xxxii. 31.

HAS the human heart ever been satisfied with false gods? Can pleasure or riches fill the soul that is empty of God? How about the atheist, the deist, the pantheist? What do they look forward to? Nothing! Man's life is full of trouble; but when the billows of affliction and disappointment are rising and rolling over them, they have no God to call upon. " They shall cry unto the gods whom they offer incense; but they shall not save them at all in the time of their trouble." Therefore I contend " their rock is not as our Rock."

March 15th.

And as Moses lifted up the serpent in the wilderness, even so must the Son of man be lifted up: that whosoever believeth in Him should not perish, but have eternal life.—John iii. 14, 15.

I HEARD of a woman once that thought there was no promise in the Bible for her; she thought the promises were for others, not for her. There are a good many of these people in the world. They think it is too good to be true that they can be saved for nothing. This woman one day got a letter, and when she opened

it she found it was not for her at all; it was
meant for another woman that had the same
name; and she had her eyes opened to the fact
that if she should find some promise in the
Bible directed to her name, she would not know
whether it meant her or some one else that bore
her name. But you know the word " WHOSO-
EVER " includes each and every one in the wide
world!

MARCH 16th.

*The carnal mind is enmity against God: for it is not
subject to the law of God, neither indeed can be.*—Romans viii. 7.

JESUS CHRIST, the purest being who ever
came to this earth to save mankind, was
crucified. I believe if Gabriel should come
down from heaven with all the glory of that
upper world, and try to save men, they would
try to blacken his character inside of a week.
The ungodly do not like the godly. The im-
pure do not like the pure. There is enmity
still. Men may cavil and discuss as much as
they like, but there is the fact. God's predic-
tion is fulfilled. The serpent shall have its
head bruised, and every man of us should do all
he can to bruise it. Our worst enemy is sin.

MARCH 17th.

Unto us was the gospel preached, as well as unto them: but the word preached did not profit them, not being mixed with faith in them that heard it.—Hebrews iv. 2.

FAITH is very important. It is the link that binds us to every promise of God—it brings us every blessing. I do not mean a *dead* faith, but a *living* faith. There is a great difference between the two. A man may tell me that ten thousand dollars are deposited in a certain bank in my name. I may believe it, but if I don't act upon it and get the money it does me no good. Unbelief bars the door and keeps back the blessing.

Some one has said there are three elements in faith—knowledge, assent, laying hold. Knowledge! A man may have a good deal of knowledge about Christ, but that does not save him. I suppose Noah's carpenters knew as much about the ark as Noah did, but they perished miserably nevertheless, because they were not in the ark. Our knowledge about Christ does not help us if we do not act upon it. But knowledge is very important. Many also assent and say—" I believe "; but that does not save them. Knowledge, assent, then laying hold: it is that last element that saves, that brings the soul and Christ together.

MARCH 18th.

And if I go and prepare a place for you, I will come again, and receive you unto Myself; that where I am, there ye may be also.—John xiv. 2, 3.

IF my wife were in a foreign country, and I had a beautiful mansion all ready for her, she would a good deal rather I should come myself and bring her to it than have me send some one else to bring her. Christ has prepared a mansion for His bride, the Church, and He promises for our joy and comfort that He will come Himself and bring us to the place He has been all this while preparing.

MARCH 19th.

Open Thou mine eyes, that I may behold wondrous things out of Thy law.—Psalm cxix. 18.

WE have a great many prayer-meetings, but there is something just as important as prayer, and that is that we read our Bibles, that we have Bible study and Bible lectures and Bible classes, so that we may get hold of the Word of God. When I pray, I talk to God, but when I read the Bible, God is talking to me; and it is really more important that God should speak to me than that I should speak to Him. I believe we should know better how to pray if we knew our Bibles better.

March 20th.

Be not deceived ; God is not mocked : for whatsoever a man soweth, that shall he also reap.—Galatians vi. 7.

THIS law is just as true in God's kingdom as in man's kingdom; just as true in the spiritual world as in the natural world. If I sow tares, I am going to reap tares; if I sow a lie, I am going to reap lies; if I sow adultery I am going to reap adulterers; if I sow whisky, I am going to reap drunkards. You cannot blot this law out, it is in force. No other truth in the Bible is more solemn.

March 21st.

Come unto Me, all ye that labor and are heavy laden, and I will give you rest.—Matthew xi. 28.

I LIKE to have a text like this, because it takes us all in. "Come unto Me ALL ye that labor." That doesn't mean a select few—refined ladies and cultured men. It doesn't mean good people only. It applies to saint and sinner. Hospitals are for the sick, not for healthy people. Do you think that Christ would shut the door in any one's face, and say, "I did not mean *all*; I only meant certain ones"? If you cannot come as a saint, come as a sinner. Only come !

A lady told me once that she was so hardhearted she couldn't come.

"Well," I said, "my good woman, it doesn't say all ye soft-hearted people come. Black hearts, vile hearts, hard hearts, soft hearts, all hearts come. Who can soften your hard heart but Himself?"

MARCH 22d.

He shall call upon thee, and I will answer Him. —Psalm xci. 15.

IF we call on God for deliverance and for victory over sin and every evil, God will not turn a deaf ear to our call. I don't care how black the life has been, I don't care what the past record has been, I don't care how disobedient or how one may have backslidden and wandered; if one really wants to come back, God accepts the willing mind, God will hear prayer, and answer.

Some people say they can't call. Perhaps you cannot make an eloquent prayer—I hope you can't—I have heard about all the eloquent prayers I want to. But you can say, " God, be merciful to me, a sinner."

Only be sincere, and God will hear your cry. Mark you, there is a sham cry. Mothers understand that; they know when their children cry in earnest, or whether it is a sham cry. Let the child give a real cry of distress, and the mother will leave everything and fly to her child. I have been forty years in Christian work, and I have never known God to disappoint any man or woman who was in earnest about their soul's salvation or were seeking a more consecrated life. I know lots of people who pretend to be in earnest, but their prayers are never answered.

MARCH 23d.

O Zion, that bringest good tidings, get thee up into the high mountains.—Isaiah xl. 9.

A TRAVELLER once made arrrangements with a guide to take him to the top of a high mountain to see the sunrise. They had not journeyed long when there arose a terrible thunderstorm. "It's no use to go on," the gentleman said. "We cannot see the sunrise in the midst of this fearful storm." "O, sir," said the guide, "we shall soon get above the storm." They could see the lightning playing about them, and the grand old mountain shook with the thunder, and it was very dark; but when they passed up above the clouds all was light and clear. So if it is dark here, rise higher; it is light enough up around the throne. If I may rise up to the light, I have no business to be in darkness. Rise higher, higher, higher. It is the privilege of the child of God to walk on unclouded.

MARCH 24th.

And suddenly, when they had looked round about, they saw no man any more, save Jesus only with themselves.—Mark ix. 8.

WHAT a dark night it would have been if 'our Lord and Master had been caught up with Moses and Elijah, and no Christ had died for our sins. Oh, how Jesus Christ has lit up this world! But suppose that He had gone up to heaven on the other side of Calvary, and had never finished His work. Suppose that God in His love for His Son had said: "I can't let those men spit upon you and smite you; I will take you back to My bosom." What darkness would have settled down on this world! But Moses disappeared, and Elijah disappeared, and Christ only was left, for Christ is all. The law and the prophets were honored and fulfilled in Him.

MARCH 25th.

I acknowledged my sin unto Thee, and mine iniquity have I not hid. I said, I will confess my transgressions unto the Lord; and Thou forgavest the iniquity of my sin.—Psalm xxxii. 5.

WE are good at confessing other people's sins, but if it is true repentance, we shall have as much as we can do to look after our own. When a man or woman gets a good look into God's looking-glass, he is not finding fault with other people: he is fully occupied at home.

March 26th.

*He shall glorify Me : for he shall receive of Mine,
and shall shew it unto you.*—John xvi. 14.

THE world can get on very well without you
and me, but the world cannot get on without Christ, and therefore we must testify of
Him.

The world to-day is just hungering and thirsting for this divine, satisfying portion. Thousands and thousands are sitting in darkness,
knowing not of this great Light, but when we
begin to preach Christ honestly, faithfully, sin-
cerely and truthfully; holding Him up, not ourselves; exalting Christ, and not our theories;
presenting Christ, and not our opinions; advo-
cating Christ, and not some false doctrine; then
the Holy Ghost will come and bear witness.
He will testify that what we say is true.

March 27th.

*Beloved, let us love one another : for love is of God;
and every one that loveth is born of God, and knoweth
God.*—1 John iv. 7.

THE first impulse of a young convert is to
love. Do you remember the day you
were converted? Was not your heart full of
sweet peace and love?

I remember the morning I came out of my
room after I had first trusted Christ. I thought

the old sun shone a good deal brighter than it
ever had before. I thought that the sun was
just smiling upon me. I walked out upon Boston Common, and heard the birds in the trees,
and I thought that they were all singing a song
for me. Do you know I fell in love with the
birds? I never cared for them before, but now
it seemed to me that I was in love with all
creation. I had not a bitter-feeling against any
man, and I was ready to take all men to my
heart. If a man has not the love of God shed
abroad in his heart, he has never been
regenerated.

MARCH 28th.

*And thou shalt take this rod in thine hand, where-
with thou shalt do signs.*—Exodus iv. 17.

WHEN God Almighty linked Himself to
that rod, it was worth more than all the
armies the world had ever seen. Look and see
how that rod did its work. It brought up the
plagues of flies, and the thunderstorm, and
turned the water into blood. It was not Moses,
however, nor Moses' rod that did the work, but
it was the God of the rod, the God of Moses.
As long as God was with him, he could not
fail.

MARCH 29th.

They shall keep My laws and My statutes in all Mine assemblies ; and they shall hallow My Sabbaths.— Ezekiel xliv. 24.

NO nation has ever prospered that has trampled the Sabbath in the dust. Show me a nation that has done this, and I will show you a nation that has got in it the seeds of ruin and decay. I believe that Sabbath desecration will carry a nation down quicker than anything else. Adam brought marriage and the Sabbath with him out of Eden, and neither can be disregarded without suffering.

MARCH 30th.

*For what shall it profit a man, if he shall gain the whole world, and lose his own soul?—*Mark viii. 36.

O THAT we would wake up to the thought of what it is to be lost! The world has been rocked to sleep by Satan, who is going up and down telling people that it doesn't mean anything. I believe in the old-fashioned heaven and hell. Christ came down to save us from a terrible hell, and any man who is cast down to hell from here must go in the full blaze of the gospel, and over the mangled body of the Son of God.

We hear of a man who has lost his health, and we sympathize with him, and we say it is very sad. Our hearts are drawn out to sympathy. Here is another man who has lost his wealth, and we say, " That is very sad." Here is another man who has lost his reputation, his standing among men. " That is sadder still," we say. We know what it is to lose health and wealth and reputation, but what is the loss of all these things compared with the loss of the soul?

MARCH 31st.

Ye shall receive power, after that the Holy Ghost is come upon you: and ye shall be witnesses unto Me, both in Jerusalem, and in all Judæa, and in Samaria, and unto the uttermost part of the earth.—Acts i. 8.

I HAVE little sympathy with the idea that Christian men and women have to live for years before they can have the privilege of leading any one out of the darkness of this world into the kingdom of God. I do not believe, either, that all God's work is going to be done by ministers, and other officers in the churches. This lost world will never be reached and brought back to loyalty to God until the children of God wake up to the fact that they have a mission in the world. If we are true Christians we shall all be missionaries. Christ came down from heaven on a mission, and if we have His Spirit in us we will be missionaries too. If we have no desire to see the world discipled, to see men brought back to God, there is something very far wrong in our religion.

APRIL 1st.

They that will be rich fall into temptation and a snare, and into many foolish and hurtful lusts, which drown men in destruction and perdition.—1 Timothy vi. 9.

THINK of Balaam. He is generally regarded as a false prophet, but I do not find that any of his prophecies that are recorded are not true; they have been literally fulfilled. Up to a certain point his character shone magnificently, but the devil finally overcame him by the bait of covetousness. He stepped over a heavenly crown for the riches and honors that Balak promised him. He went to perdition backward. His face was set toward God, but he backed into hell. He wanted to die the death of the righteous, but he did not live the life of the righteous. It is sad to see so many who know God, miss everything for riches.

APRIL 2d.

If we confess our sins, He is faithful and just to forgive us our sins, and to cleanse us from all unrighteousness.—1 John i. 9.

THERE may be some confessions we need to make to be brought into close fellowship with God. We must coöperate with God. You may take a bottle and cork it up tight, and put it under Niagara, and not a drop of that mighty volume of water will get into the bottle.

If there is any sin in my heart that I am not willing to confess and to give up, I need not expect a blessing. The men who have had power with God in prayer have always begun by confessing their sins. Take the prayers of Jeremiah and Daniel. We find Daniel confessing his sin, when there isn't a single sin recorded against him.

April 3d.

Thou shalt not make unto Thee any graven image, or any likeness of anything that is in heaven above, or that is in the earth beneath, or that is in the water under the earth.—Exodus xx. 4.

I WOULD a great deal sooner have five minutes' communion with Christ than spend years before pictures and images of Him. Whatever comes between my soul and my Maker is not a help to me, but a hindrance. God has given different means of grace by which we can approach Him. Let us use these, and not seek for other things that He has distinctly forbidden.

April 4th.

Then said these men, We shall not find any occasion against this Daniel, except we find it against him concerning the law of his God.—Daniel vi. 5.

WHAT a testimony from his bitterest enemies! Would that it could be said of all of us! He had never taken a bribe, he had never been connected with a "ring." Ah, how his name shines! He had commenced to shine in his early manhood, and he shone right along. Now he is an old man, an old statesman, and yet this is their testimony.

Character is worth more than money. Character is worth more than anything else in the wide world. I would rather in my old age have such a character as that which Daniel's enemies gave him than have raised over my dead body a monument of gold reaching from earth to sky.

April 5th.

And He said unto me, My grace is sufficient for thee: for my strength is made perfect in weakness. Most gladly therefore will I rather glory in my infirmities, that the power of Christ may rest upon me.—2 Corinthians xii. 9.

WHEN we are weak then we are strong. People often think they have not strength enough; the fact is we have too much strength. It is when we feel that we have no strength of our own, that we are willing God should use us, and work through us. If we are leaning on God's strength, we have more than all the strength of the world.

April 6th.

Having made peace through the blood of His cross. . . .—Colossians i. 20.

A GREAT many people are trying to make their peace with God, but that has already been done. God has not left it for us to do; all that we have to do is to enter into it, to accept it. It is a condition, and instead of our trying to make peace and to work for peace, we want to cease all that, and simply enter into peace that has been purchased for us.

April 7th.

I will be with him in trouble.—Psalm xci. 15.

IT is a great thing to have a place of resort in the time of trouble. How people get on without the God of the Bible is a mystery to me. If I didn't have such a refuge, a place to go and pour out my heart to God in such times, I don't know what I would do. It seems as if I would go out of my mind. But to think, when the heart is burdened, we can go and pour it into His ear, and then have the answer come back, "I will be with Him," there is comfort in that!

I thank God for the old Book. I thank God for this old promise. It is as sweet and fresh to-day as it has ever been. Thank God, none of those promises are out of date, or grown stale. They are as fresh and vigorous and young and sweet as ever.

April 8th.

In My Father's house are many mansions: if it were not so, I would have told you. I go to prepare a place for you.—John xiv. 2.

WHAT has been, and is now, one of the strongest feelings in the human heart? Is it not to find some better place, some lovelier spot, than we now have? It is for this that men everywhere are seeking, and they can have it if they will; but instead of looking down, they must look *up* to find it. As men grow in knowledge, they vie with each other more and more in making their homes attractive, but the brightest home on earth is but an empty barn compared with the mansions Jesus has gone to prepare.

April 9th.

I will arise and go to my father, and will say unto him, Father I have sinned against heaven, and before thee.—Luke xv. 18.

ONE of the greatest battles ever fought was being fought out then. Everything holy and heavenly was beckoning the prodigal home. The powers of darkness were trying to keep him from returning.

"You go back and they'll all laugh at you. What'll they say?" said the devil.

No doubt there was an angel hovering over

him, watching for the decision, and when he said, " I will arise, " the angel bore it on high.

" Make another crown. Get another robe ready. There's another sinner coming! "

That "I will" echoed and reëchoed, and there was joy in the presence of the angels. He is saved. His heart has got home already. The battle with pride and sin is over.

APRIL 10th.

For I say unto you, Ye shall not see Me henceforth, till ye shall say, Blessed is He that cometh in the name of the Lord.—Matthew xxiii. 39.

WHEN Christ returns, He will not be treated as He was before. There will be room for Him at Bethlehem. He will be welcome in Jerusalem. He will reveal Himself as Joseph revealed himself to his brethren. He will say to the Jews, "I am Jesus," and they will reply : "Blessed is He that cometh in the name of the Lord." And the Jews will then be that nation that shall be born in a day.

APRIL 11th.

Ye shall seek Me and find Me when ye shall search for Me with all your heart.—Jeremiah xxix. 13.

THESE are the men who find Christ—those who seek for Him *with all their heart.* I am tired and sick of half-heartedness. You don't like a half-hearted man, you don't care for any one to love you with a half-heart ; and the Lord won't have it. If we are going to seek for Him and find Him, we must do it with all our heart.

I believe the reason why so few people find Christ is because they are not *terribly* in earnest about their soul's salvation. *God* is in earnest ; everything He has done proves that He is in earnest about the salvation of men's souls. What is Calvary but a proof of that? And the Lord wants us to be in earnest when it comes to this great question of the soul's salvation. I never saw men seeking Him with all their hearts but they soon found Him.

APRIL 12th.

Watch and pray, that ye enter not into temptation : the spirit indeed is willing, but the flesh is weak.— Matthew xxvi. 41.

THE flesh is weak. Is there any one on earth that dares to dispute that statement? Is there anything weaker under the sun than the human flesh? The spirit is willing. Most men would rather do the right thing, and think they will do it. Tell them that they will do certain things inside of twelve months, and they would say, as the king did, "Is thy servant a dog that he should do such a thing? No, never." But they will do it just the same. " The spirit is willing, but the flesh is weak. "

APRIL 13th.

The Lord bless thee and keep thee.—Numbers vi. 24.

GOD can do what He has done before. He kept Joseph in Egypt; Moses before Pharaoh; Daniel in Babylon; and enabled Elijah to stand before Ahab in that dark day. And I am so thankful that these I have mentioned were men of like passions with ourselves.

APRIL 14th.

He that heareth My word, and believeth on Him that sent Me, hath everlasting life.—John v. 24.

A MAN once prayed for me that I might obtain eternal life *at last.* I could not have said " Amen " to that. I obtained eternal life over forty years ago, when I was converted. What is the "gift of God," if it is not eternal life? And what makes the gospel such good news? Is it not that it offers eternal life to every poor sinner who will take it?

APRIL 15th.

Lo, I see four men loose, walking in the midst of the fire.—Daniel iii. 25.

IT does my heart good to think that the worst the devil can do is to burn off the bonds of God's children. If Christ be with us, the worst afflictions can only loosen our earthly bonds, and set us free to soar higher.

April 16th.

Prepared as a bride, adorned for her husband.—
Revelation xxi. 2.

THERE are constant sounds around us that we cannot hear, and the sky is studded with bright worlds that our eyes have never seen. Little as we know about this bright and radiant land, there are glimpses of its beauty that come to us now and then.

Perhaps nothing but the shortness of our range of sight keeps us from seeing the celestial gates all open to us, and nothing but the deafness of our ears prevents our hearing the joyful ringing of the bells of heaven.

April 17th.

He that heareth My word, and believeth on Him that sent Me, . . . shall not come into judgment.—
John v. 24.

IN a prairie fire, when the wind is strong, the wall of flame often rolls along twenty feet high, destroying man and beast in its onward rush. The frontiersmen know they cannot run as fast as that fire. Not the fleetest horse can escape it. But they just take a match, and light the grass before them. These flames sweep a space, and men follow and take their stand in the burned district, and are safe. Over the place where they stand the fire has already passed, and there is nothing left to burn. So there is one spot on earth that the judgment of God has swept over. Eighteen hundred years ago the storm burst on Calvary; and the Son of God endured it: and now, if we take our stand by the Cross, we are safe for time and for eternity.

April 18th.

He made haste and came down, and received Him joyfully.—Luke xix. 6.

DID you ever hear of any one receiving Christ in any other way? He received Him *joyfully*. Christ brings joy with Him. Sin, gloom, and darkness flee away; light, peace, and joy burst into the soul.

April 19th.

Go ye into all the world, and preach the gospel to every creature.—Mark xvi. 15.

I CAN imagine Jesus saying: "Go search out the man who put that crown of thorns on My brow; tell him I will have a crown for him in My kingdom, if he will accept salvation; and there shall not be a thorn in it. Find out that man who took the reed from My hand, and smote My head, driving the thorns deeper into My brow. Tell him I want to give him a sceptre. Go, seek out that poor soldier who drove the spear into My side; tell him that there is a nearer way to My heart than that. Tell him I want to make him a soldier of the Cross, and that My banner over him shall be love."

April 20th.

I can do all things through Christ which strengthneth me.—Philippians iv. 13.

TAKE Christ for your strength, dear soul. He'll give you power. Power to overcome the world, the flesh, and the devil; power to crucify every besetting sin, passion, lust; power to shout in triumph over every trouble and temptation of your life, "I can do all things through Christ which strengtheneth me."

April 21st.

One man of you shall chase a thousand.—Joshua xxiii. 10.

WHEN in Glasgow, a friend was telling me about a man who was preaching one Sabbath morning on Shamgar. He said: "I can imagine that when he was ploughing in the field a man came running over the hill all out of breath, and shouted: 'Shamgar! Shamgar! There are six hundred Philistines coming toward you.' Shamgar quietly said: 'You pass on; I can take care of them, they are four hundred short.' So he took an ox goad and slew the whole of them. He routed them hip and thigh." "One shall chase a thousand." Nowadays it takes about a thousand to chase one, because we do not realize that we are weak in ourselves and that our strength is in God.

APRIL 22d.

Exceeding great and precious promises.—2 Peter i. 4.

LET men feed for a month on the promises of God and they will not be talking their "leanness." It is not leanness, it is laziness. There is an abundant supply for us if we will only rouse ourselves to take it.

APRIL 23d.

From darkness unto light.—Acts xxvi. 18.

I REMEMBER one night when the Bible was the driest and darkest book in the universe to me. The next day it was all light. I had the key to it. I had been born of the Spirit. But before I knew anything of the mind of God in His word I had to give up my sin.

APRIL 24th.

A kingdom which shall never be destroyed.—Daniel ii. 4.

NAPOLEON tried to establish a kingdom by the force of arms. So did Alexander the Great, and Cæsar, and other great warriors; but they utterly failed. Jesus founded His kingdom on love, and it is going to stand. When we get on to this plane of love, then all selfish and unworthy motives will disappear, and our work will stand the fire when God shall put it to the test.

April 25th.

And in every work that He began, He did it with His heart.—2 Chronicles xxxi. 21.

IN all ages God has used those who were in earnest. Satan always calls idle men into his service. God calls active and earnest—not indolent men. You remember where Elijah found Elisha ploughing in the field. Gideon was at the threshing floor. Moses was away in Horeb looking after the sheep. None of these were indolent men; what they did, they did with all their might. We want such men and women nowadays. If we cannot do God's work with all the knowledge we would like, let us at any rate do it with all the zeal that God has given us.

April 26th.

For the zeal of Thine house hath eaten me up.— Psalm lxix. 9.

I HEARD of some one who was speaking the other day of something that was to be done, and who said he hoped zeal would be tempered with moderation. Another friend very wisely replied that he hoped moderation would be tempered with zeal. If that were always the case, Christianity would be like a red hot ball rolling over the face of the earth. There is no power on earth that can stand before the onward march of God's people when they are in dead earnest.

April 27th.

I would thou wert cold or hot.—Revelation iii. 15.

WHAT we want is to be red hot all the time. Do not wait until some one hunts you up. People talk about striking while the iron is hot. I believe it was Cromwell who said that he would rather strike the iron and make it hot. So let us keep at our post, and we will soon grow warm in the Lord's work.

April 28th.

He shall show you things to come.—John xvi. 13.

PEOPLE talk about news nowadays. The Bible is the only news-book in the world. The newspaper tells us what *has* taken place, but this Book tells us what *will* take place. And for people to be shutting it up, and saying we can be guided without it, is just as reasonable as to shut out the sun by closing up our windows because we have the electric light. There is as much reason to say that the sun is worn out as to say that we have got beyond the Bible.

April 29th.

It is written.—Matthew iv. 4, 7, 10.

CHRIST overcame Satan by the word. He simply said: " It is written "; and a second time, and a third time, " It is written "; and that was the arrow that shot right into him and drove him away. The devil does not care a bit about our feelings. He can make our feelings good or bad; he can take us up on the mountain, or down into the valley, and we can only vanquish him by the sword of the Spirit, which is the Word.

APRIL 30th.

I knew a man in Christ above fourteen years ago, (whether in the body, I cannot tell; or whether out of the body, I cannot tell, God knoweth;) such an one caught up to the third heaven.—2 Corinthians xii. 2.

SOME people have wondered what the third heaven means. That is where God dwells, and where the storms do not come. There sits the incorruptible Judge. Paul, when he was caught up there, heard things that it was not lawful for him to utter, and he saw things that he could not speak of down here. The higher up we get in spiritual matters, the nearer we seem to heaven. There our wishes are fulfilled at last.

MAY 1st.

Our conversation is in heaven.—Philippians iii. 20.

SOME one asked a Scotchman if he was on the way to heaven, and he said: "Why man, I live there; I am not on the way." That is just it. We want to *live* in heaven; while we are walking in this world it is our privilege to have our hearts and affections there.

May 2d.

It is high time to awake out of sleep.—Romans xiii. 11.

AS I have said, there are a great many in the church who make one profession, and that is about all you hear of them; and when they come to die you have to go and hunt up some musty old church records to know whether they were Christians or not. God won't do that. What we want is men with a little courage to stand up for Christ. When Christianity wakes up, and every child that belongs to the Lord is willing to speak for Him, is willing to work for Him, and, if need be, willing to die for Him, then Christianity will advance, and we shall see the work of the Lord prosper.

May 3d.

Verily, verily, I say unto you, He that heareth My word, and believeth on Him that sent Me, hath everlasting life, and shall not come into condemnation, but is passed from death unto life.—John v. 24.

I WOULD a thousand times rather stand on that verse than all the frames and feelings I ever had. I took my stand there twenty years ago. Since then the dark waves of hell have come dashing up against me; the waves of persecution have broken all around me; doubts, fears, and unbelief in turn have assailed me; but I have been able to stand firm on this short word of God. It is a sure footing for eternity.

MAY 4th.

There is joy in the presence of the angels of God over one sinner that repenteth.—Luke xv. 10.

" JOY in the *presence* of the angels?" Perhaps the friends who have left the shores of time may be looking down upon us; and when they see one they prayed for while on earth turning to God, it sends a thrill of joy to their very hearts. Even now, some mother who has gone up yonder may be looking down upon a son or daughter, and if that child should say : " I will meet that mother of mine; I will decide for God," the news, with the speed of a sunbeam, reaches heaven, and that mother may then rejoice, as we read, " In the presence of the angels."

MAY 5th.

All . . . all . . . all.—Matthew xxviii. 17–20.

ALL *power* is given unto Me ; go *teach all* nations. Teach them what ? To *observe all* things. There are a great many people now that are willing to observe what they like about Christ, but the things that they don't like they turn away from. But His commission to His disciples was, " Go teach all nations to observe all things whatsoever I have commanded you." And what right has a messenger who has been sent of God to change the message ?

MAY 6th.

And they were all filled with the Holy Ghost.—Acts ii. 4.

IN Exodus we read that when Moses had finished the Tabernacle in the desert, the Shekinah came and filled it with the presence of God—that was the Holy Spirit. The moment the tabernacle was ready it was filled. And when the Temple was built, and the priests and the Levites were there singing with one accord, the cloud came and filled the Temple; the moment the Temple was ready it was filled.

These were two of His dwelling places; but where does He dwell now? Ye are the temples for the Holy Spirit to dwell in, and the moment the heart is ready, the Spirit of God will fill it.

MAY 7th.

Will ye also go away? . . . Lord, to whom shall we go?—John vi. 67, 68.

THE sun is thousands of years old, but gas is new. Shall we then use gas in place of the sun? Block up all the windows of your houses, and have nothing to do with the sun! You might as well do that as give up the Bible. Outgrown it! Why, there is no book to be compared with it. No other book will lift up the world. If you could go into a town where men were trying to live without that good book, **you would flee from it as they who left Sodom** and Gomorrah. Have infidels ever produced a Knox, a Bunyan, or a Milton ?

MAY 8th.

Have not I sent thee ?—Judges vi. 14.

GOD knows and you know what He has sent you to do. God sent Moses to Egypt to bring three millions of bondmen up out of the house of bondage into the promised land. Did he fail ? It looked, at first, as if he were going to. But did he ? God sent Elijah to stand before Ahab, and it was a bold thing for him to say there should be neither dew nor rain : but did He not lock up the heavens for three years and six months ?

But did he fail ? And you cannot find any place in Scripture where a man was ever sent by God to do a work in which he failed.

MAY 9th.

He being dead, yet speaketh.—Hebrews xi. 4.

BUT there is one thing you cannot bury with a good man ; his influence still lives. They have not buried Daniel yet ; his influence is as great to-day as ever it was. Do you tell me that Joseph is dead ? His influence still lives and will continue to live on and on. You may bury the frail tenement of clay that a good man lives in, but you cannot get rid of his influence and example. Paul was never more powerful than he is to-day.

MAY 10th.

Your joy no man taketh from you.—John xvi. 22.

IN the second century, they brought a martyr before a king, and the king wanted him to recant and give up Christ, but the man spurned the thought. The king said : "If you don't do it, I will banish you." The man smiled and answered : "You can't banish me from Christ. He says He will never leave me nor forsake me." The king got angry, and said : "Well, I will confiscate your property and take it all from you." And the man replied : "My treasures are laid up on high; you cannot get them." The king became still more angry, and said : "I will kill you." "Why," the man answered, "I have been dead forty years; I have been dead with Christ; dead to the world. My life is hid with Christ in God, and you cannot touch it." And so we can rejoice, because we are resurrection ground, having risen with Christ. Let persecution and opposition come. "Your joy no man taketh from you."

MAY 11th.

Lord, what wilt Thou have me to do?—Acts ix. 6.

A MAN at sea was once very seasick. If there is a time when a man feels that he cannot do any work it is then. But he heard that a man had fallen overboard. He couldn't do much, but he laid hold of a light and held it up to the porthole. The light fell on the drowning man's hand, and a man caught him, and pulled him into the lifeboat. It seemed a small thing to do to hold up the light; yet it saved the man's life. We can do as much as that. If we cannot do some great thing we can hold the light for some poor, perishing soul, who is out in the dark waters of sin.

May 12th.

I believe God, that it shall be even as it was told me.—Acts xxvii. 25.

FAITH is a belief in testimony. It is not a leap in the dark. God does not ask any man to believe without giving him something to believe. You might as well ask a man to see without eyes, as to bid him believe without giving him something to believe.

May 13th.

God is Love.—1 John iv. 8.

IF I could only make men understand the real meaning of the words of the Apostle John— " GOD IS LOVE."— I would take that single text, and would go up and down the world proclaiming this glorious truth. If you can convince a man that you love him you have won his heart. If we could really make people believe that God loves them, how we should find them crowding

into the kingdom of heaven! The trouble is
that men think God hates them; and so they
are continually turning their backs on Him.

MAY 14th.

What is that in thine hand?—Exodus iv. 2.

HERE was Moses a weak solitary man going
down to Egypt, to meet a monarch who
had the power of life and death. And all he
had with which to deliver the people from bondage was this rod! Yet see how famous that
rod became. God's servant had but to stretch
it out, and the water of the country was turned
into blood. He had only to lift up the rod and the
waters of the Red Sea separated, so that the
people could pass through dry-shod. He lifted
this rod and struck the flinty rock, when the
water burst forth, and they drank and were re-
freshed. That contemptible rod became mighty
indeed. But it was not the rod; it was the
God of Moses, who condescended to use it.

MAY 15th.

The law is our schoolmaster to bring us to Christ.—
Galatians iii. 24.

DOCTRINES are to the soul what the streets
which lead to the house of a friend who
has invited me to dinner are to the body. They
will lead me there if I take the right one; but
if I remain in the streets my hunger will never

be satisfied. Feeding on doctrines is like trying to live on dry husks; and lean indeed must the soul remain which will not partake of the Bread sent down from heaven.

MAY 16th.

There shall be no more death.—Revelation xxi. 4.

SOME one said to a person dying: "Well, you are in the land of the living yet." "No," said he, "I am in the land of the dying, but I am going to the land of the living; they live there and never die." This is the land of sin and death and tears, but up yonder they never die. It is perpetual life; it is unceasing joy.

MAY 17th.

Eye hath not seen, nor ear heard, neither hath it entered into the heart of man, the things which God hath prepared for them that love Him.—Isaiah lxiv. 4.

But God hath revealed them unto us by His spirit.— 1 Corinthians ii. 10.

MOST people say "eye hath not seen, nor ear heard," and they stop there. But see what the New Testament says, "God hath revealed them unto us by His Spirit." You see the Lord hath revealed them unto us: "For the Spirit searches all things—yea, the deep things of God."

MAY 18th.

Hitherto have ye asked nothing in My name. Ask and ye shall receive.—John xvi. 24.

IT is related of Alexander that he gave one of his generals, who had pleased him, permission to draw on his treasurer for any sum. When the draft came in, the treasurer was scared, and would not pay it till he saw his master. And when the treasurer told him what he had done, Alexander said, " Don't you know that he has honored me and my kingdom by making a large draft ? " So we honor God by making a large draft on Him.

MAY 19th.

Which is the earnest of our inheritance.—Ephesians i. 14.

A POOR woman once told Rowland Hill that the way to heaven was short, easy and simple ; comprising only three steps—out of self, into Christ, and into glory. We have a shorter way now—out of self and into Christ. That is heaven begun below—a little of what waits us over there.

MAY 20th.

Now then, do it.—2 Samuel iii. 18.

I REMEMBER hearing of a man in one of the hospitals who received a bouquet of flowers from the Flower Mission. He looked at the beautiful bouquet and said: "Well, if I had known that a bunch of flowers could do a fellow so much good, I would have sent some myself when I was well." If people only knew how they might cheer some lonely heart and lift up some drooping spirit, or speak some word that shall be lasting in its effects for all coming time, they would be up and about it.

MAY 21st.

Our Father.—Matthew vi. 9.

IF you ask me why God should love us, I cannot tell. I suppose it is because He is a true Father. It is His nature to love; just as it is the nature of the sun to shine.

MAY 22d.

I will fasten Him as a nail in a sure place; . . . and they shall hang upon Him all the glory of His Father's house, the offspring and the issue, all vessels of small quantity, from the vessels of cups, even to all the vessels of flagons.—Isaiah xxii. 23, 24.

THERE is one nail, fastened in a sure place; and on it hang all the flagons and all the cups. "Oh," says one little cup, "I am so small and so black, suppose I were to drop!" "Oh," says a flagon, "there is no fear of you; but I am so heavy, so very weighty, suppose I were to drop!" And a little cup says, "Oh, if I were only like the gold cup there, I should never fear falling." But the gold cup answers, " It is not because I am a gold cup that I keep up; but because I hang upon the nail."

May 23d.

Let your light so shine before men, that they may see your good works and glorify your Father which is in heaven.—Matthew v. 16.

IF a man has not grace to keep his temper, he is not fit to work for God. If he cannot live uprightly at home, he is not fit for God's service; and the less he does the better. But he *can* keep his temper, he *can* live uprightly at home, by the grace of God.

May 24th.

I have fought a good fight.—2 Timothy iv. 7.

ROME never had such a conqueror as Paul within her walls. Rome never had such a mighty man as Paul within her boundaries. Although the world looked down upon him, and perhaps he looked very small and contemptible, yet in the sight of heaven he was the mightiest man who ever trod the streets of Rome. Probably there will never be another one like him travelling those streets. The Son of God walked with him, and the form of the fourth was with him.

MAY 25th.

The blood of Jesus Christ, His Son, cleanseth us from all sin.—1 John i. 7.

YOU may pile up your sins till they rise like a dark mountain, and then multiply them by ten thousand for those you cannot think of: and after you have tried to enumerate all the sins you have ever committed, just let me bring this one verse in, and that mountain will melt away.

MAY 26th.

Not without flood.—Hebrews ix. 7.

LOOK at the Roman soldier as he pushed his spear into the very heart of the God-man. What a hellish deed! But what was the next thing that took place? Blood covered the spear! Oh! thank God, the blood covers sin. The very crowning act of sin brought out the crowning act of love; the crowning act of wickedness was the crowning act of grace.

MAY 27th.

Nor idolaters . . . shall inherit the kingdom of God.—1 Corinthians vi. 9, 10.

IT is clear that idolaters are not going to enter the kingdom of God. I may make an idol of my business; I may make an idol of the wife of my bosom; I may make idols of my children. I do not think you need go to heathen countries to find men guilty of idolatry. Anything that comes between me and God is an idol—anything, I don't care what it is; business is all right in its place, and there is no danger of my loving my family too much if I love God more; but God must have the first place; and if He has not, then the idol is set up.

MAY 28th.

As many as received Him, to them gave He power to become the sons of God.—John i. 12.

BY receiving Him you get power, and not otherwise. Many persons have tried to be Christians, and have failed. A man may as well try to jump to Europe, as to try to serve God before he is born of God. He has not the power. But when he receives Christ, Christ is the power of God unto salvation. We take Him: and He is our salvation.

MAY 29th.

I will seek that which was lost.—Ezekiel xxxiv. 16.

I DO not believe there is a man that the Spirit of God has not striven with at some period of his life. Bear in mind, Christ takes the place of the seeker. Every man who has ever been saved through these six thousand years was sought after by God. No sooner did Adam fall, than God sought him. He had gone away frightened, and hid himself away among the bushes in the garden, but God sought him; and from that day to this, God has always had the place of the Seeker.

MAY 30th.

O thou of little faith, wherefore didst thou doubt ?— Matthew xiv. 31.

SOME one has said: " There are three ways to look. If you want to be wretched, look within; if you wish to be distracted, look around; but if you would have peace, look up." Peter looked away from Christ, and he immediately began to sink. He had God's eternal word, which was sure footing, and better than either marble, granite or iron; but the moment he took his eyes off Christ down he went.

MAY 31st.

Ye shine as lights.—Philippians ii. 15.

IF we cannot be a lighthouse, let us be a tallow candle. In the old times, people used to come to the evening meetings, bringing their candles with them. The first one would not make a great illumination, but as more came there was more light. Suppose all Christians to-day were burning with even a candle light, would not God be more glorified? If we cannot be a lighthouse let us be a tallow candle. Or even a farthing rushlight! That is well enough if it is all you can be. Be all you can.

JUNE 1st.

*My reward is with Me, to give every man according
as his work shall be.*—Revelation xxii. 12.

IF I understand things correctly, whenever you
find men or women who are looking to be
rewarded here for doing right, they are unquali-
fied to work for God; because if they are looking for the applause of men, looking for reward
in this life, it will disqualify them for the service
of God.

JUNE 2d.

*Lay up for yourselves treasures in heaven ; for where
your treasure is, there will your heart be also.*—Matthew vi. 20.

VERY few people are satisfied with earthly
riches. Often the richer the man the
greater the poverty. Somebody has said that
getting riches brings care; keeping them brings
trouble; abusing them brings guilt; and losing
them brings sorrow. It is a great mistake to
make so much of riches as we do. But there
are some riches that we cannot praise too much :
that never pass away. They are the treasures
laid up in heaven for those who truly belong to
God.

JUNE 3d.

Waxed strong through faith.—Romans iv. 20. (R. V.)

REAL true faith is man's weakness leaning on
God's strength. It is the Shepherd's business to keep the sheep. Who ever heard of the

sheep keeping the shepherd? People have an idea that they have to keep themselves and Christ too. It is a false idea. It is the work of the Shepherd to look after them, and take care of those who trust Him. An Irishman said, on one occasion, that he often trembled, but his Rock never did.

JUNE 4th.

Arise ye and depart, for this is not your rest.—Micah ii. 2.

THIS world that some think is heaven, is the home of sin, a hospital of sorrow, a place that has nothing in it to satisfy the soul. Men go all over it and then want to get out of it. The more men see of the world the less they think of it. People soon grow tired of the best pleasures it has to offer. Some one has said that the world is a stormy sea, whose every wave is strewed with the wrecks of mortals that perish in it. Every time we breathe some one is dying. We all know that we are going to stay here but a very little while. Only the other life is enduring.

JUNE 5th.

Who is on the Lord's side?—Exodus xxxii. 26.

WHEN I was in England in 1867, a friend happened to introduce me to a man from Dublin. Alluding to me, the latter said, " Is this young man all O O?" Said the London man, "What do you mean by O O?" Replied the Dublin man, "*Is he Out-and-Out for Christ?*" I tell you it burned down into my soul. It means a good deal to be O O for Christ.

JUNE 6th.

Now we see through a glass darkly; but then face to face.—1 Corinthians xiii. 12.

THE word Paul used, properly translated, is "mirror." Now, we see God, as it were, in a mirror, but then, face to face.

Suppose we knew nothing of the sun except what we saw of its light reflected from the moon? Would we not wonder about its immense distance, about its dazzling splendor, about its life-giving power? But all that we see, the sun, the moon, the stars, the ocean, the earth, the flowers, and above all, man, are a grand mirror in which the perfection of God is imperfectly reflected.

JUNE 7th.

Ye are not under law but under grace.—Romans vi. 14.

WHEN Moses was in Egypt, to punish Pharaoh he turned the waters into blood. When Chirst was on earth He turned the water into wine. That is the difference between law and grace. The law says, " Kill him "; grace says, " Forgive him." Law says, " Condemn him "; grace says, " Love him." When the law came out of Horeb three thousand men were destroyed. (Ex. xxxii. 28.) At Pentecost, under grace, three thousand men found life. (Acts ii. 41.) What a difference! When Moses came to the burning bush, he was commanded to take the shoes from off his feet. When the prodigal came home after sinning he was given a pair of shoes to put on his feet. I would a thousand times rather be under grace than under the law.

JUNE 8th.

Everlasting joy.—Isaiah xxxv. 2.

I THINK there is a difference between happiness and joy. *Happi*-ness is caused by things which *happen* around me, and circumstances will mar it, but joy flows right on through trouble; joy flows on through the dark; joy flows in the night as well as in the day; joy flows all through persecution and opposition; it is an unceasing fountain bubbling up in the heart: a secret spring which the world can't see and don't know anything about. The Lord gives His people perpetual joy when they walk in obedience to Him.

June 9th.

Arise, shine.—Isaiah lx. 1.

LOVE must be active, as light must shine. As some one has said: "A man may hoard up his money ; he may bury his talents in a napkin ; but there is one thing he cannot hoard up, and that is love." You cannot bury it. It *must* flow out. It cannot feed upon itself ; it must have an object.

June 10th.

Wilt thou not tell.—Ezekiel xxiv. 19.

WE may not be able to do any great thing ; but if each of us will do *something*, however small it may be, a good deal will be accomplished for God. For many years I have made it a rule not to let any day pass without speaking to some one about eternal things. I commenced it away back years ago, and if I live the life allotted to man, there will be more than eighteen thousand persons who will have been spoken to personally by me. How often we as Christians meet with people, when we might turn the conversation into a channel that will lead them up to Christ.

June 11th.

And things which are despised, hath God chosen.
—1 Corinthians i. 28.

NOTICE that all the men whom Christ called around Him were weak men in a worldly sense. They were all men without rank, without title, without position, without wealth or culture. Nearly all of them were fishermen and unlettered men; yet Christ chose them to build up His kingdom. When God wanted to bring the children of Israel out of bondage, He did not send an army; He sent one solitary man. So in all ages God has used the weak things of the world to accomplish His purposes.

June 12th.

Yea the faith that is by Him, hath given him this perfect soundness.—Acts iii. 16.

FAITH is the hand that takes the blessing. But don't look too much at the hand. Suppose I ask a man who has just received a thousand dollars of a friend : " Did he give it to you with his right hand ? " He would reply : "What do I care about which hand; so that I have got the money."

June 13th.

To every man his work.—Mark xiii. 34.

IF you notice that verse carefully it does not read "to every man some work," or "to every man a work," but "to every man *his* work." And I believe that every man and woman living has a work laid out for them to do; that every man's life is a plan of the Almighty, and that away back in the councils of eternity God laid out a work for every one of us. There is no man living who can do the work that God has for me to do, no one but myself. And if any man's work is not done, he will have to answer for it when he stands before the bar of God.

June 14th.

The Lord will give grace and glory.—Psalms lxxxiv. 11.

THERE is not such a great difference between grace and glory after all. Grace is the bud, and glory the blossom. Grace is glory begun, and glory is grace perfected. It will not come hard to people who are serving God down here to do it when they go up yonder. They will change places, but they will not change employments.

June 15th.

The things which are seen are temporal; but the things which are not seen are eternal.—2 Corinthians iv. 18.

THE heir to some great estate, while a child, thinks more of a dollar in his pocket than all his inheritance. So even some professing Christians are more elated by a passing pleasure than they are by their title to eternal glory.

June 16th.

Faith without works is dead.—James ii. 20.

YOU may very often see dead fish floating with the stream, but you never saw dead fish swimming against it. Well, that is your false believer. Profession is just floating down the stream, but *con*fession is swimming against it, no matter how strong the tide.

June 17th.

Blessed are ye when men . . . persecute you.—Matthew v. 4.

LISTEN to Paul in the jail at Philippi. "If God wants me to go to heaven by way of this prison," he says, "it is all the same to me; rejoice and be exceeding glad, Silas. I thank God that I am accounted worthy to suffer for Jesus' sake." And as they sang their praises to

God, the other prisoners heard them; but, what
was far more important, the Lord heard them,
and the old prison shook. Talk about Alexander the Great making the world tremble with
his armies. Here is a little tent-maker who
makes the world tremble without any army!

JUNE 18th.

I am the light of the world.—John vii. 12.

I HEARD of an infidel once who said, "Look
at your convert; it is all moonshine." The
young convert replied to him, "I thank you for
the compliment. We are perfectly willing to
be called that. The moon borrows the light
from the sun, and so we borrow ours from
Christ."

JUNE 19th.

*Though He was rich yet for your sakes He became
poor.*—2 Corinthians viii. 9.

THIS poor world is groaning and sighing for
sympathy—human sympathy. I am quite
sure it was that in Christ's life which touched
the hearts of the common people. He made
Himself one with them. He who was rich for
our sakes became poor. He was born in the
manger so that He might put Himself on a level
with the lowest of the low.

JUNE 20th.

Take ye away the stone.—John xi. 39.

BEFORE the act of raising Lazarus could be performed, the disciples had their part to do. Christ could have removed the stone with a word. It would have been very easy for Him to have commanded it to roll away, and it would have obeyed His voice, as the dead Lazarus did when He called him back to life. But the Lord would have His children learn this lesson: that they have something to do toward raising the spiritually dead. The disciples had not only to take away the stone, but after Christ had raised Lazarus they had to " loose and let him go."

JUNE 21st.

Like the troubled sea, when it cannot rest.—Isaiah lvii. 20.

THE only thing that can keep us from peace is sin. God turneth the way of the wicked upside down. There is no peace for the wicked, saith my God. They are like the troubled sea that cannot rest, casting up filth and mire all the while; but peace with God by faith in Jesus Christ—peace through the knowledge of forgiven sin, is like a rock; the waters go dashing and surging past, but it abides.

June 22d.

Do good . . . hoping for nothing again.—Luke vi. 35.

LOVE never looks to see what it is going to get in return. I have generally found that those workers who are all the time looking to see how much they are going to get from the Lord are never satisfied. But love does its work and makes no bargain.

June 23d.

Born again, not of corruptible seed but of incorruptible.—1 Peter i. 23.

GOD has not only adopted us, but we are His by birth: we have been born into His kingdom. My boy was as much mine when he was a day old as now that he is fourteen. He was *my son;* although it did not appear what he would be when he attained manhood. He is mine; although he may have to undergo probation under tutors and governors. The children of God are not perfect; but we are perfectly His children.

June 24th.

Now faith is the substance of things hoped for, the evidence of things not seen.—Hebrews xi. 1.

THIS is the Bible definition of Faith. The best definition I ever saw outside the Bible is: Dependence on the veracity of another. In other words, Faith says Amen to everything that God says. Faith takes God without any " If 's." If God says it, Faith says, " I believe it "; Faith says " Amen " to it.

June 25th.

So we see that they could not enter in because of unbelief.—Hebrews iii. 19.

WHEN the Israelites first came out of Egypt God would have led them right up into the land of Canaan if it had not been for their accursed unbelief. But they desired something besides God's word; so they were turned back, and had to wander in the desert for forty years. I believe there are thousands of God's children wandering in the wilderness still. The Lord has delivered them from the hand of the Egyptian, and would at once take them through the wilderness right into the Promised Land, if they were only willing to follow Christ. Christ has been down here, and has made the rough places smooth, and the dark places light, and the crooked places straight. If we will only be led by Him right into the land of promise, all will be peace, and joy, and rest.

June 26th.

I rejoiced greatly when the brethren testified of the truth that is in thee.—3 John i. 3.

THERE is more than one kind of joy; there is the joy of one's own salvation. I thought, when I first tasted that, it was the most delicious joy I had ever known, and that I could never get beyond it. But I found, afterward, there was something more joyful than that, the joy of the salvation of others. Oh, the privilege, the blessed privilege, to be used of God to win a soul to Christ, and to see a man or woman being led out of bondage by some act of ours. To think that God should condescend to allow us to be co-workers with Him! It is the highest honor we can have. It surpasses the joy of our own salvation, this joy of seeing others saved, and walking in the truth.

JUNE 27th.

They looked unto Him and were lightened.—Psalm xxxiv. 5.

IF you want to scatter your doubts, look at the blood; and if you want to increase your doubts, look at yourself. You will get doubts enough for years by being occupied with yourself only a few days.

JUNE 28th.

We give thanks to God and the Father of our Lord Jesus Christ . . . for the hope which is laid up for you in heaven.—Colossians i. 3, 5.

A GREAT many persons imagine that anything said about heaven is only a matter of speculation. They talk about heaven much as they would about the air. Now there would not have been so much in Scripture on this subject if God had wanted to leave the human race in darkness about it. "All Scripture," we are told, "is given by inspiration of God, and is profitable for doctrine, for reproof, for correction, for instruction in righteousness, that the man of God may be perfect—thoroughly furnished unto all good works." What the Bible says about heaven is just as true as what it says about everything else. The Bible is inspired. What we are taught about heaven could not have come to us in any other way than by inspiration. No one knew anything about it but God, and so if we want to find out anything about it we have to turn to His word.

June 29th.

But to him that worketh not, but believeth on him that justifieth the ungodly, his faith is counted unto him for righteousness.—Romans iv. 5.

THE thief had nails through both hands, so that he could not work; and a nail through each foot, so that he could not run errands for the Lord: he could not lift a hand or a foot toward his salvation; and yet Christ offered him the gift of God, and he took it. He threw him a passport, and took him with Him into paradise.

June 30th.

But the fruit of the Spirit is love, joy, peace, long-suffering, gentleness, faith, meekness, goodness, temperance : against such there is no law.—Galatians v. 22, 23.

THE fruit of the Spirit begins with love. There are nine graces spoken of, and of these nine Paul puts love at the head of the list; love is the first thing, the first in that precious cluster of fruit. Some one has said that all the other eight can be put in terms of love. Joy is love exulting; peace is love in repose; long-suffering is love on trial; gentleness is love in society; goodness is love in action; faith is love on the battlefield; meekness is love at school; and temperance is love in training. So it is love all the way; love at the top, love at the bottom, and all the way along down this list of graces. If we only just brought forth the fruit of the Spirit, what a world we would have ! Men would have no desire to do evil.

July 1st.

Be ye doers of the word, and not hearers only, deceiving your own selves.—James i. 22.

A MAN may preach with the eloquence of an angel, but if he don't live what he preaches, and act out in his home and his business what he professes, his testimony goes for naught, and the people say it is all hypocrisy, it is all a sham. Words are very empty if there is nothing back of them. Your testimony is poor and worthless if there is not a record back of it consistent with what you profess.

What we need is to pray to God to lift us up out of this low, cold, formal state that we have been living in, that we may live in the atmosphere of God continually, and that the Lord may lift upon us the light of His countenance, and that we may shine in this world, reflecting His grace and glory.

July 2d.

They that know Thy name will put their trust in Thee: for Thou, Lord, hast not forsaken them that seek Thee.—Psalm ix. 10.

A MAN will not trust strangers. I want to get acquainted with a man before I put my confidence in him. I have known God for forty years, and I have more confidence in Him now than I ever had before; it increases every year. In the Bible, some things that were dark ten years ago are plain to-day; and some things that are dark now will be plain ten years hence.

We must take things by faith. You take the existence of cities on the testimony of men that have been in those cities; and we ask men to take our testimony, who have found joy in believing.

July 3d.

And I give unto them eternal life; and they shall never perish, neither shall any man pluck them out of My hand. My Father, which gave them Me, is greater than all; and no man is able to pluck them out of My Father's hand. I and My Father are one.—John x. 28, 29, 30.

THESE are precious verses to those who are afraid of falling, who fear that they will not hold out. It is God's work to hold. It is the Shepherd's business to keep the sheep. Whoever heard of the sheep going to bring back the shepherd? People have an idea that they have to keep themselves and Christ too. It is a false idea. It is the work of the Shepherd to look after them, and to take care of those who trust Him. He has promised to do it.

A sea captain, when dying said, "Glory to God, the anchor holds." He trusted in Christ. His anchor had taken hold of the solid Rock.

July 4th.

And He did not many mighty works there because of their unbelief.—Matthew xiii. 58.

UNBELIEF is as much an enemy to the Christian as it is to the unconverted. It will keep back the blessing now as much as it did in the days of Christ. We read that in one place Christ could not do many mighty works because of unbelief. If Christ could not do this, how can *we* expect to accomplish anything if the people of God are unbelieving? I contend that God's children are alone able to hinder God's work. Infidels, atheists, and sceptics cannot do it. Where there is union, strong faith, and expectation among Christians, a mighty work is always done.

July 5th.

If the wicked restore the pledge, give again that he had robbed, walk in the statutes of life, without committing iniquity; he shall surely live, he shall not die. None of his sins that he hath committed shall be mentioned unto him: he hath done that which is lawful and right; he shall surely live.—Ezekiel xxxiii. 15, 16.

IF you have ever taken money dishonestly, you need not pray God to forgive you and fill you with the Holy Ghost until you make restitution. If you have not got the money now to pay back, will to do it, and God accepts the willing mind.

Many a man is kept in darkness and unrest because he fails to obey God on this point. If the plough has gone deep, if the repentance is true, it will bring forth fruit. What use is there in my coming to God until I am willing, like Zacchæus, to make it good, if I have done any man wrong or have taken anything from him falsely? Confession and restitution are the steps that lead up to forgiveness.

July 6th.

Thou shalt have no other gods before me.—Exodus xx. 3.

YOU don't have to go to heathen lands to-day to find false gods. America is full of them. Whatever you make most of is your god. Whatever you love more than God is your idol. Many a man's heart is like some Kaffirs' huts, so full of idols that there is hardly room to turn around. Rich and poor, learned and unlearned, all classes of men and women are guilty of this sin. "The mean man boweth down, and the great man humbleth himself."

A man may make a god of himself, of a child, of a mother, of some precious gift that God has bestowed upon him. He may forget the Giver, and let his heart go out in adoration toward the gift. "Thou shalt have *no* other gods before me."

July 7th.

Then came Peter to Him, and said, Lord, how oft shall my brother sin against me, and I forgive him? till seven times? Jesus saith unto him, I say not unto thee, Until seven times: but, Until seventy times seven.—Matthew xviii. 21, 22.

PETER did not seem to think that *he* was in danger of falling into sin; his question was, How often should I forgive *my brother?* But very soon we hear that Peter has fallen. I can imagine that when he did fall, the sweet thought came to him of what the Master had said.

The voice of sin may be loud, but the voice of forgiveness is louder.

JULY 8th.

So also is the resurrection of the dead. It is sown in corruption, it is raised in incorruption: it is sown in dishonor, it is raised in glory: it is sown in weakness, it is raised in power: it is sown a natural body, it is raised a spiritual body.—1 Corinthians xv. 42–44.

AS I go into a cemetery I like to think of the time when the dead shall rise from their graves. We read part of this chapter in what we call the " burial service." I think it is an unfortunate expression. Paul never talked of " burial." He said the body was *sown* in corruption, *sown* in weakness, *sown* in dishonor, *sown* a natural body. If I *bury* a bushel of wheat, I never expect to see it again, but if I *sow* it, I expect results. Thank God, our friends are not buried; they are only sown ! I like the Saxon name for the cemetery—" God's acre."

JULY 9th.
There is no difference, for all have sinned, and come short of the glory of God.—Romans iii. 22, 23.

THAT is one of the hardest truths man has to learn. We are apt to think that we are just a little better than our neighbors, and if we find *they* are a little better than ourselves, we go to work and try to pull them down to our level. If you want to find out who and what man is, go to the third chapter of Romans, and there the whole story is told. " There are none righteous, no, not one." " All have sinned and come short." *All!* Some men like to have their lives written before they die. If you would like to read your biography, turn to this chapter, and you will find it already written.

July 10th.

Come unto Me, all ye that labor and are heavy laden, and I will give you rest.—Matthew xi. 28.

SOME years ago a gentleman asked me which I thought was the most precious promise of all those that Christ left. I took some time to look over the promises, but I gave it up. I found that I could not answer the question. Like a man with a large family of children, he cannot tell which he likes best, he loves them all. But if not the best, this is one of the sweetest promises of all :

" Come unto Me, all ye that labor and are heavy laden, and I will give you rest. Take My yoke upon you, and learn of Me, for I am meek and lowly in heart : and ye shall find rest unto your souls. For My yoke is easy, and My burden is light."

July 11th.

He that covereth his sins shall not prosper: but whoso confesseth and forsaketh them shall have mercy. —Proverbs xxviii. 13.

" HE that covereth his sins shall not prosper." He may be a man in the pulpit, a priest before the altar, a king on the throne; I don't care who he is. Man has been trying it for six thousand years. Adam tried it, and failed. Moses tried it when he buried the Egyptian whom he killed, but he failed. " Be sure your sin will find you out." You cannot bury your sin so deep but it will have a resurrection by and by, if it has not been blotted out by the Son of God. What man has failed to do for six thousand years, we had better give up trying to do.

July 12th.

For we wrestle not against flesh and blood, but against principalities, against powers, against the rulers of the darkness of this world, against spiritual wickedness in high places.—Ephesians vi. 12.

THE reason why so many Christians fail all through life is just this—they under-estimate the strength of the enemy. We have a terrible enemy to contend with. Don't let Satan deceive us. Unless we are spiritually dead, it means warfare. Nearly everything around tends to draw us away from God. We do not step clear out of Egypt on to the throne of God. There is the wilderness journey, and there are enemies in the land.

July 13th.

Be clothed with humility: for God resisteth the proud, and giveth grace to the humble.—1 Peter v. 5.

A MAN can counterfeit love, he can counterfeit faith, he can counterfeit hope and all the other graces, but it is very difficult to counterfeit humility. You soon detect mock humility. They have a saying among the Arabs that as the tares and the wheat grow they show which God has blessed. The ears that God has blessed bow their heads and acknowledge every grain, and the more fruitful they are the lower their heads are bowed. The tares lift up their heads erect, high above the wheat, but they are only fruitful of evil.

If we only get down low enough, God will use us to His glory.

July 14th.

The love of Christ constraineth us.—2 Corinthians v. 14.

I AM getting sick and tired of hearing the word *duty, duty*. You hear so many talk about it being their duty to do this and do that. My experience is that such Christians have very little success. Is there not a much higher plat-

form than that of mere duty ? Can we not en-
gage in the service of Christ because we love
Him ? When that is the constraining power
it is so easy to work.

It is not hard for a mother to watch over a
sick child. She does not look upon it as any
hardship. You never hear Paul talking about
what a hard time he had in his Master's service.
He was constrained by love to Christ, and by
the love of Christ to him. He counted it a
joy to labor, and even to suffer, for his blessed
Master.

JULY 15th.

*For Christ also hath once suffered for sins, the just
for the unjust, that He might bring us to God, being
put to death in the flesh, but quickened by the Spirit.—*
1 Peter iii. 18.

HERE we see that Christ was raised up from
the grave by the Spirit, and the power ex-
ercised to raise Christ's dead body must raise
our dead souls and quicken them. No other
power on earth can quicken a dead soul but the
same power that raised the body of Jesus Christ
out of Joseph's sepulchre. And if we want that
power to quicken our friends who are dead in
sin, we must look to God, and not be looking
to man to do it. If we look alone to ministers,
if we look alone to Christ's disciples to do this
work, we shall be disappointed; but if we look

to the Spirit of God and expect it to come from Him and Him alone, then we shall honor the Spirit, and the Spirit will do His work.

JULY 16th.

There are three that bear record in heaven, the Father, the Word, and the Holy Ghost, and these three are one.—1 John v. 7.

BY the Father is meant the first Person, Christ, the Word is the second, and the Holy Spirit, perfectly fulfilling His own office and work in union with the Father and the Son, is the third. I find clearly presented in my Bible, that the One God who demands my love, service and worship, has there revealed Himself, and that each of those three names of Father, Son and Holy Ghost has personality attached to them. Therefore we find some things ascribed to God as Father, some to God as Saviour, and some to God as Comforter and Teacher. It has been remarked that the Father plans, the Son executes, and the Holy Spirit applies. But I also believe they plan and work together.

JULY 17th.

Pray without ceasing.—1 Thessalonians v. 17.

IT was in November or December when those men of Judah arrived at Sheeshan (Nehemiah i. 1, 2), and Nehemiah prayed on until March or April before he spoke to the king.

If a blessing doesn't come to-night, pray harder to-morrow, and if it doesn't come to-morrow, pray harder, and even then, if it doesn't come, keep right on, and you will not be disappointed. God in heaven will hear your prayers, and will answer them. He has *never failed*, if a man has been honest in his petitions and honest in his confessions. Let your faith beget patience. God is never in a hurry, said St. Augustine, because He has all eternity to work.

JULY 18th.

God is not a man, that He should lie; neither the son of man, that He should repent: hath He said, and shall He not do it? or hath He spoken, and shall He not make it good?—Numbers xxiii. 19.

SUPPOSE a man, in directing me to the post office, gives me ten landmarks, and that in my progress there I find nine of them to be as he told me. I should have good reason to believe that I was coming to the post office.

And if, by believing, I get a new life, and a hope, a peace, a joy, and a rest to my soul that I never had before; if I get self-control, and find that I have a power to resist evil and to do good, I have pretty good proof that I am on the right road to the " city which hath foundations, whose builder and maker is God." And if things have taken place, and are now taking place, as recorded in God's Word, I have good reason to conclude that what yet remains will be fulfilled. And yet people talk of doubting! Faith is to take God at His word, unconditionally.

July 19th.

I will set Him on high.—Psalm xci. 14.

GOD is able to do it. Up above the angels, up above the archangels, up above the cherubims and seraphims, on the throne with His own Son.

We are called to be sons and daughters of the eternal God. Do you know, the Prince of Wales cannot sit on the throne with Queen Victoria? But it is not so yonder. Christ has gone up and taken His seat at the right hand of the Father, and every son and daughter of God is to be lifted up to the throne. Think of the promise. Isn't it rich, isn't it sweet? "I will set Him on high."

July 20th.

And the Lord turned, and looked upon Peter. And Peter remembered the word of the Lord, how He had said unto him, Before the cock crow, thou shalt deny Me thrice. And Peter went out and wept bitterly.—Luke xxii. 61, 62.

THE Master might have turned and said to Peter, "Is it true, Peter, that you have forgotten Me so soon? Do you not remember when your wife's mother lay sick of a fever that

I rebuked the disease and it left her? Do you not call to mind your astonishment at the draught of fishes so that you exclaimed, 'Depart from me; for I am a sinful man, O Lord'? Do you remember when in answer to your cry, 'Lord, save me, or I perish,' I stretched out My hand and kept you from drowning in the water? Have you forgotten when, on the Mount of Transfiguration, with James and John, you said to me, 'Lord, it is good to be here: let us make three tabernacles.' Have you forgotten being with Me at the supper-table, and in Gethsemane? Is it true that you have forgotten Me so soon?" The Lord might have upbraided him with questions such as these; but He did nothing of the kind. He cast one look on Peter, and there was so much love in it that it broke that bold disciple's heart, and he went out and wept bitterly.

JULY 21st.

He must increase, but I must decrease.—John iii. 30.

DOCTOR BONAR once remarked that he could tell when a Christian was growing. In proportion to his growth in grace he would elevate his Master, talk less of what he was doing, and become smaller and smaller in his own esteem, until, like the morning star, he faded away before the rising sun. Jonathan was willing to decrease that David might increase; and John the Baptist showed the same spirit of humility.

JULY 22d.

I will be with Him in trouble.—Psalm xci. 15.

WE are apt to think that young people do not have any trouble, but if they haven't, there is one thing they can make sure of, that they are going to have trouble later. " Man is born unto trouble, as the sparks fly upward." Trouble is coming. No one is exempt. God has had one Son without sin, but He has never had one without sorrow. Jesus Christ, our Master, suffered as few men ever suffered, and He died very young. Ours is a path of sorrow and suffering, and it is so sweet to hear the Master say :

" I will be with you in trouble."

Don't think for a moment that you can get on without Him. You may say now, " I can get on; I am in good health and prosperity," but the hour is coming when you will need Him.

JULY 23d.

I am not ashamed of the gospel of Christ: for it is the power of God unto salvation to every one that believeth.—Romans i. 16.

I REMEMBER some meetings being held in a locality where the tide did not rise very quickly, and bitter and reproachful things were being said about the work. But one day, one of the most prominent men in the place rose and said:

"I want it to be known that I am a disciple of Jesus Christ; and if there is any odium to be cast on His cause, I am prepared to take my share of it."

It went through the meeting like an electric current, and a blessing came at once to his own soul and to the souls of others.

July 24th.

After these things the word of the Lord came unto Abram in a vision, saying, Fear not, Abram: I am thy shield, and thy exceeding great reward.— Genesis xv. 1.

ABRAM might have thought that the kings that he had defeated might get other kings and other armies to come, and he might have thought of himself as a solitary man, with only three hundred and eighteen men, so that he might have feared lest he be swept from the face of the earth. But the Lord came and said:

"Abram, fear not."

That is the first time those oft-repeated words "Fear not" occur in the Bible.

"Fear not, for I will be your shield and your reward."

I would rather have that promise than all the armies and all the navies of the world to protect me—to have the God of heaven for my Protector! God was teaching Abram that He was to be his Friend and his Shield, if he would surrender himself wholly to His keeping, and trust in His goodness. That is what we need—to surrender ourselves up to God, fully and wholly.

July 25th.

God so loved the world, that He gave His only begotten Son, that whosoever believeth in Him should not perish, but have everlasting life.—John iii. 16.

I HAVE never been able to preach from that text. I have often thought I would, but it is so high that I can never climb to its height, I have just quoted it and passed on. Who can fathom the depth of those words: "God *so* loved the world"? We can never scale the heights of His love or fathom its depths. Paul prayed that he might know the height, the depth, the length, and the breadth, of the love of God; but it was past his finding out.

July 26th.

Let me die the death of the righteous, and let my last end be like his!—Numbers xxiii. 10.

THE sanctified man and the unsanctified one look at heaven very differently. The unsanctified man simply chooses heaven in preference to hell. He thinks that if he must go to either one he would rather try heaven. It is like a man with a farm who has a place offered him in another country, where there is said to be a gold mine; he hates to give up all he has and take any risk. But if he is going to be banished, and must leave, and has his choice of living in a wilderness or digging in a coal pit, or else take the gold mine, then there is no hesitation. The unregenerate man likes heaven better than hell, but he likes this world the best of all. The true believer prizes heaven above everything else, and is always willing to give up the world. Everybody wants to enjoy heaven after they die, but they don't want to be heavenly-minded while they live.

JULY 27th.

Let your light so shine before men, that they may see your good works, and glorify your Father which is in heaven.—Matthew v. 16.

WE see very few illuminated Christians. If every one of us was illuminated by the Spirit of God, how we could light up the churches! But to have a lantern without any light, would be a nuisance. Many Christians carry along lanterns and say, "I wouldn't give up my religion for yours." They talk about religion. The religion that has no fire is like painted fire. These are artificial Christians.

Do you belong to that class? You can tell. If you can't, your friends can.

July 28th.

She hath done what she could: she is come aforehand to anoint My body to the burying.—Mark xiv. 8.

I IMAGINE when Mary died, if God had sent an angel to write her epitaph, he couldn't have done better than to put over her grave what Christ said:

"She hath done what she could."

I would rather have that said over my grave, if it could honestly be said, than to have all the wealth of the Rothschilds. Christ raised a monument to Mary that is more lasting than the monuments raised to Cæsar or Napoleon. Their monuments crumble away, but hers endures. Her name never appeared in print while she was on earth, but to-day it is famous in three hundred and fifty languages.

We may never be great; we may never be known outside our circle of friends; but we may, like Mary, do what we can. May God help each one of us to do what we can! Life will soon be over; it is short at the longest. Let us rise and follow in the footsteps of Mary of Bethany.

July 29th.

Give us day by day our daily bread.—Luke xi. 3.

IF God could set a table for His people in the wilderness, and feed three millions of Israelites for forty years, can He not give us our daily bread? I do not mean only the bread that perisheth, but also the Bread that cometh from above. If He feeds the birds of the air, surely He will feed His children made in His own image! If He numbers the very hairs of our head, He will take care to supply all our temporal wants.

JULY 30th.

For all things are for your sakes, that the abundant grace might through the thanksgiving of many redound to the glory of God. For which cause we faint not; but though our outward man perish, yet the inward man is renewed day by day.—2 Corinthians iv. 15, 16.

A MAN can no more take in a supply of grace for the future than he can eat enough to-day to last him for the next six months, or take sufficient air into his lungs at once to sustain life for a week to come. We must draw upon God's boundless stores of grace from day to day, as we need it.

JULY 31st.

And I appoint unto you a kingdom, as My Father hath appointed unto Me; that ye may eat and drink at My table in My kingdom, and sit on thrones judging the twelve tribes of Israel.—Luke xxii. 29, 30.

THINK of the Lord stooping down and taking a poor drunkard right up and out of the gutter, and putting his feet on the rock, and a new song in his mouth, and lifting him up

above powers and principalities, above angels
and archangels, seraphims and cherubims, up,
up, up, on to the throne with Himself! Do you
suppose that an angel flying over the nations of
the earth would look at any throne? What a
great time they had a few years ago putting the
Czar on to the throne of Russia! Nation after
nation sent representatives to assist at the cere-
monies. But Christ's is more than that. His
is an everlasting kingdom. His is a throne that
is going to endure forever; and He says, " Ye
shall sit with Me on My throne." Man, look
up! Look at the stars to-night! Our inheritance is above.

AUGUST 1st.

*So shall My word be that goeth forth out of My
mouth: it shall not return unto Me void, but it shall
accomplish that which I please, and it shall prosper in
the thing whereto I sent it.*—Isaiah lv. 11.

SOMETIMES it looks as if God's servants
fail. When Herod beheaded John the
Baptist, it looked as if John's mission was a
failure. But was it? The voice that rang
through the valley of the Jordan rings through
the whole world to-day. You can hear its echo
upon the mountains and the valleys yet, "I
must decrease, but He must increase." He
held up Jesus Christ and introduced Him to the
world, and Herod had not power to behead

Him until His life-work had been accomplished.

Stephen never preached but one sermon that we know of, and that was before the Sanhedrim; but how that sermon has been preached again and again all over the world! Out of his death probably came Paul, the greatest preacher the world has seen since Christ left this earth. If a man is sent by Jehovah, there is no such thing as failure.

AUGUST 2d.

And I will make of thee a great nation, and I will bless thee, and make thy name great; and thou shalt be a blessing.—Genesis xii. 2.

THERE is no name in history so well known as the name of Abram. Even Christ is not more widely known, for the Mohammedans, the Persians, and the Egyptians make a great deal of Abram. His name has been for centuries and centuries favorably known in Damascus. God promised him that great men should spring from his loins. Was there ever a nation that has turned out such men? Think of Moses, and Joseph, and Joshua, and Caleb, and Samuel, and David, and Solomon, and Elisha. Think of Elijah, and Daniel, and Isaiah, and all the other wonderful Bible characters that have sprung from this man! Then think of John the Baptist, of Peter, of James, and John, and Paul, a mighty army. No one can number the multitude of wonderful men that have sprung from this one man called out of the land of the Chaldeans, unknown and an idolater, probably, when God called him; and yet how literally God has fulfilled His promise that through him He would bless all the nations of the earth. All because he surrendered himself fully and wholly to let God bless him.

AUGUST 3th.

And when they could not come nigh unto Him for the press, they uncovered the roof where He was: and when they had broken it up, they let down the bed wherein the sick of the palsy lay.—Mark ii. 4.

THESE four friends were terribly in earnest. They let the bier, on which the man was lying, down into the room. They laid their friend right at the feet of Jesus Christ; a good place to lay him, was it not?

Perhaps you have a sceptical son or an unbelieving husband, or some other member of your family, that scoffs at the Bible and sneers at Christianity. Lay them at the feet of Jesus, and He will honor your faith.

AUGUST 4th.

Vanity of vanities, saith the preacher ; all is vanity. Ecclesiastes xii. 8.

THE worship of pleasure is slavery. (Solomon tried pleasure, and found bitter disappointment, and down the ages has come the bitter cry, "All is vanity.")

There is no rest in sin. The wicked know nothing about rest. The Scriptures tell us the wicked "are like the troubled sea that cannot rest." Man, like the sea, has no rest. He has had no rest since Adam fell, and there is none for him until he returns to God again, and the light of Christ shines into his heart.

Rest cannot be found in the world, but thank God the world cannot take it from the believing heart! Sin is the cause of all this unrest. It brought toil and labor and misery into the world.

AUGUST 5th.

Know ye not that the unrighteous shall not inherit the kingdom of God? Be not deceived: neither fornicators, nor idolaters, nor adulterers, nor effeminate, nor abusers of themselves with mankind, nor thieves, nor covetous, nor drunkards, nor revilers, nor extortioners, shall inherit the kingdom of God.—1 Corinthians vi. 9, 10.

NOTICE that the covetous are named between thieves and drunkards. We lock up thieves, and have no mercy on them. We loathe drunkards, and consider them great sinners against the law of God as well as the law of the land. Yet there is far more said in the Bible against covetousness than against either stealing or drunkenness.

August 6th.

Now when the congregation was broken up, many of the Jews and religious proselytes followed Paul and Barnabas: who, speaking to them, persuaded them to continue in the grace of God.—Acts xiii. 43.

HOW much would Paul and Barnabas have accomplished if they had pronounced the benediction and sent these people home? It is a thing to weep over that we have got thousands and thousands of church-members who are good for nothing toward extending the kingdom of God. They understand bazaars, and fairs, and sewing-circles; but when you ask them to sit down and show a man or woman the way into God's kingdom, they say:

"Oh, I am not able to do that. Let the deacons do it, or some one else."

It is all wrong. The Church ought to be educated on this very point. There are a great many church-members who are just hobbling about on crutches. They can just make out that they are saved, and imagine that is all that constitutes a Christian in this nineteenth century. As far as helping others is concerned, that never enters their heads. They think if they can get along themselves, they are doing amazingly well. They have no idea what the Holy Ghost wants to do through them.

August 7th.

Many will say to Me in that day, Lord, Lord, have we not prophesied in Thy name? and in Thy name have cast out devils? and in Thy name done many wonderful works? And then will I profess unto them, I never knew you: depart from Me, ye that work iniquity.—Matthew vii. 22, 23.

IT has been said that there will be three things which will surprise us when we get to heaven—one, to find many whom we did not expect to find there; another, to find some not there whom we had expected; a third, and perhaps the greatest wonder, to find ourselves there!

August 8th.

The wind bloweth where it listeth, and thou hearest the sound thereof, but canst not tell whence it cometh, and whither it goeth: so is every one that is born of the Spirit.—John iii. 8.

YOU might just as well tell me that there is no such thing as wind, as tell me there is no such thing as a man being born of the Spirit. I have felt the Spirit of God working in my heart just as really and as truly as I have felt the wind blowing in my face. I cannot reason it out. There are a great many things I cannot reason out, but which I believe. I never could reason out the creation. I can see the world, but I cannot tell how God made it out of nothing. But every man will admit there was a creative power.

AUGUST 9th.

Awake thou that sleepest, and arise from the dead, and Christ shall give thee light.—Ephesians v. 14.

IF the lost are to be reached by the gospel of the Son of God, Christianity must be more aggressive than it has been in the past. We have been on the defensive long enough; the time has come for us to enter on a war of aggression. When we as children of God wake up and go to work in the vineyard, then those who are living in wickedness all about us will be reached; but not in any other way. You may go to mass meetings and discuss the question: "How to reach the masses," but when you have done with discussion you have to go back to personal effort. Every man and woman who loves the Lord Jesus Christ must wake up to the fact that he or she has a mission in the world, in this work of reaching the lost.

AUGUST 10th.

Then said Jesus, Let her alone : against the day of My burying hath she kept this.—John xii. 7.

I CAN imagine that Mary thought that if she waited until Jesus was dead she might not have a chance to anoint His body, and so she came before His death to anoint Him.

There is a lesson there. How very kind and thoughtful we are to a family that has lost some member, and what kind words are said after the person is dead and gone! Would it not be better to say a few of those good things before they go? Wouldn't it be well to give some of your bouquets before a man dies, and not go and load down his coffin?

AUGUST 11th.

But Daniel purposed in his heart that he would not defile himself with the portion of the king's meat, nor with the wine which he drank: therefore he requested of the prince of the eunuchs that he might not defile himself.—Daniel i. 8.

I CAN imagine men saying to Daniel, "Look here, young man, you are too puritanical. Don't be too particular; don't have too many religious scruples. Bear in mind you are not now in Jerusalem. You will have to get over these notions, now you are here in Babylon. You are not now surrounded by friends and relatives. You are not a Jerusalem prince now. You have been brought down from your high position. You are now a captive. And if the monarch hears about your refusing to eat the same kind of meat that he eats, and to drink the same kind of wine that he drinks, your head will soon roll from off your shoulders. You had better be a little politic."

But this young man had piety and religion deep down in his heart; and that is the right place for it; where it will grow; where it will have power; where it will regulate the life. Daniel had not joined the company of the faithful few in Jerusalem because he wanted to get into " society," and attain a position: it was because of the love he had toward the Lord God of Israel.

AUGUST 12th.

And Jacob awakened out of his sleep, and he said, Surely the Lord is in this place; and I knew it not. And he was afraid, and said, How dreadful is this place! this is none other but the house of God, and this is the gate of heaven.—Genesis xxviii. 16, 17.

WHEN people come into the house of God they put on a sober appearance. They act as if there was something very strange about the house of God.

I would not say a word to detract from the holiness of the house of God. But let us bear in mind that every place ought to be holy to a child of God ; that in every place we ought to be true to God. We ought to be as true to Him in our place of business as we are in the Church. When Jacob said, " This is the house of God, and this is the gate of heaven," he was under the canopy of high heaven. That was where God met him; and God will meet us in the street as well as in the place of worship. He will meet us at home. He is also with us in our closets.

Any place where God is is holy, and this putting on another air and a sanctimonious look when we come into the house of God, and laying it aside when we go out, thinking that this is going to be acceptable to God, is all wrong. Every place ought to be holy to a true child of God.

AUGUST 13th.

But as it is written, Eye hath not seen, nor ear heard, neither have entered into the heart of man, the things which God hath prepared for them that love Him. But God hath revealed them unto us by His Spirit: for the Spirit searcheth all things, yea, the deep things of God.—1 Corinthians ii. 9, 10.

IT is said by travellers that in climbing the Alps the houses of far distant villages can be seen with great distinctness, so that sometimes the number of panes of glass in a church window can be counted. The distance looks so short that the place to which the traveller is journeying appears almost at hand, but after hours and hours of climbing it seems no nearer. This is because of the clearness of the atmosphere. By perseverance, however, the place is reached at last, and the tired traveller finds rest.

So sometimes we dwell in high altitudes of

grace; heaven seems very near, and the hills of Beulah are in full view. At other times the clouds and fogs caused by suffering and sin cut off our sight. We are just as near heaven in the one case as we are in the other, and we are just as sure of gaining it if we but keep in the path that Christ has pointed out.

AUGUST 14th.

And the Lord said unto Gideon, By the three hundred men that lapped will I save you, and deliver the Midianites into thine hand: and let all the other people go every man unto his place.—Judges vii. 7.

IT would be a good thing for the Church of God if all the fearful and faithless ones were to step to the rear, and let those who are full of faith and courage take their empty pitchers and go forward against the enemy. The little band of three hundred men who were left with Gideon routed the Midianites, but it was not their own might that gave them the victory. It was "the sword of the Lord and of Gideon." If we go on in the Name of the Lord, and trusting to His might, we shall succeed.

AUGUST 15th.

These things have I spoken unto you, that My joy might remain in you, and that your joy might be full.—John xv. 11.

PEOPLE should look for joy in the Word, and not in the world. They should look for the joy which the Scriptures furnish, and

then go to work in the vineyard; because a joy
that don't send me out to some one else, a joy
that don't impel me to go and help the poor
drunkard, a joy that don't prompt me to visit
the widow and the fatherless, a joy that don't
cause me to go into the Mission Sunday-school
or other Christian work, is not worth having,
and is not from above. A joy that does not
constrain me to go and work for the Master, is
purely sentiment and not real joy.

AUGUST 16th.

*Ye shall receive power, after that the Holy Ghost is
come upon you: and ye shall be witnesses unto Me both
in Jerusalem, and in all Judæa, and in Samaria, and
unto the uttermost part of the earth.*—Acts i. 8.

IF these early Christians had gone out and
commenced preaching then and there without
the promised power, do you think that scene
would have taken place on the day of Pentecost?
Peter would have stood up and beat against
the air, while the Jews would have gnashed
their teeth and mocked at him. But they
tarried in Jerusalem; they waited ten days.

" What!" you say, " with the world perishing and men dying! Shall I wait?"

Do what God tells you. There is no use
in running before you are sent; there is no use
in attempting to do God's work without God's

power. A man working without this unction, a man working without this anointing, a man working without the Holy Ghost upon him, is losing time after all. We shall not lose anything if we tarry till we get this power.

AUGUST 17th.

To the law and to the testimony; if they speak not according to this word, it is because there is no light in them.—Isaiah viii. 20.

ANY man, any woman who comes to us with any doctrine that is not according to the law and the testimony, let us understand that they are from the evil one, and that they are enemies of righteousness. They have no light in them. You will find these people who are consulting familiar spirits, first and last, attack the Word of God. They don't believe it.

There is another passage which reads, " And when they shall say unto you, seek unto them that have familiar spirits, and unto wizards that peep and mutter: Should not a people seek unto their God? for the living to the dead? " What is that but table-rapping, and cabinet-hiding? If it was a message from God, do you think you would have to go into a dark room and put out all the lights? In secret my Master taught nothing. God is not in that movement, and we want, as children of God, to keep ourselves from this evil.

And Nathanael said unto him, Can there any good thing come out of Nazareth? Philip saith unto him, Come and see.—John i. 46.

AFTER all, we do not gain much by discussion. Let objectors or inquirers only get one personal interview with the Son of God, and that will scatter all their darkness, all their prejudice, and all their unbelief. The moment that Philip succeeded in getting Nathanael to Christ, the work was done.

Except a man be born again, he cannot see the kingdom of God.—John iii. 3.

YOU may see many countries; but there is one country—the land of Beulah, which John Bunyan saw in vision—you shall never behold, unless you are born again, regenerated by Christ. You can look abroad and see many beautiful trees; but the tree of life you shall never behold, unless your eyes are made clear by faith in the Saviour. You may see the beautiful rivers of the earth, you may ride upon their bosoms; but bear in mind that your eye will never rest upon the river which bursts out from the Throne of God and flows through the upper Kingdom, unless you are born again. You may see the kings and lords of the earth; but the King of kings and Lord of lords you will never see except you are born again. When you are in London you may go to the Tower and see the crown of England, which is worth thousands of dollars, and is guarded by soldiers; but bear in mind that your eye will never rest upon the crown of life, except you are born again.

You may hear the songs of Zion which are sung here; but one song—that of Moses and the Lamb—the uncircumcised ear shall never hear: its melody will only gladden the ear of those who have been born again. You may look upon the beautiful mansions of earth; but bear in mind the mansions which Christ has gone to prepare you shall never see unless you are born again. It is God who says it. You may see ten thousand beautiful things in this world; but the city that Abraham caught a glimpse of— and from that time became a pilgrim and sojourner—you shall never see unless you are born again. (Heb. xi. 8, 10–16.) You may often be invited to marriage feasts here; but you will never attend the marriage supper of the Lamb except you are born again. It is God who says it.

August 20th.

Let him that thinketh he standeth, take heed lest he fall.—1 Corinthians x. 12.

TWENTY-FIVE years ago—and for the first five years after I was converted—I used to think that if I were able to stand for twenty years I need fear no fall. But the nearer you get to the Cross the fiercer the battle. Satan aims high. He went amongst the twelve, and singled out the treasurer, Judas Iscariot, and the chief apostle, Peter.

Most men who have fallen have done so on the strongest side of their character. I am told that the only side upon which Edinburgh Castle was successfully assailed was where the rocks were steepest, and where the garrison thought themselves secure. If any man thinks that he is strong enough to resist the evil at any one point he needs special watch there, for the tempter comes that way.

AUGUST 21st.

They brought young children to Him, that He should touch them : and His disciples rebuked those that brought them.—Mark x. 13.

I HAVE no sympathy with the idea that our children have to grow up before they are converted. Once I saw a lady with three daughters at her side, and I stepped up to her and asked her if she was a Christian.

"Yes, sir."

Then I asked the oldest daughter if she was a Christian. Her chin began to quiver, and the tears came into her eyes, and she said :

"I wish I was."

The mother looked very angrily at me and

said, " I don't want you to speak to my children
on that subject. They don't understand."
And in great rage she took them away from me.
One daughter was fourteen years old, one
twelve, and the other ten, but they were not old
enough to be talked to about religion! Let
them drift into the world and plunge into
worldly amusements, and then see how hard it
is to reach them. Many a mother is mourning
to-day because her boy has gone beyond her
reach. In those early days when his mind was
tender and young, she might have led him to
Christ.

August 22d.

Behold, all souls are Mine; as the soul of the father,
so also the soul of the son is Mine: the soul that sinneth,
it shall die.—Ezekiel xviii. 4.

SUPPOSE there was a law that man should
not steal, but no penalty was attached to
stealing, some man would have my pocketbook
before the day was over. If I threatened to
have him arrested, he would snap his fingers in
my face. He would not fear the law, if there
was no penalty. It is not the law that people
are afraid of; it is the penalty for transgression.

Do not suppose God has made a law without
a penalty. What an absurd thing it would be!
The penalty for sin is death: " the soul that
sinneth, it shall die." If I have sinned I must

die, or get somebody to die for me. If the Bible doesn't teach that, it doesn't teach anything. And that is where the atonement of Jesus Christ comes in.

August 23d.

These things have I spoken unto you, that ye should not be offended. They shall put you out of the synagogues : yea, the time cometh, that whosoever killeth you will think that he doeth God service.—John xvi. 1, 2.

A MAN said to me some time ago: " Mr. Moody, now that I am converted, have I to give up the world ? "

" No," said I, " you haven't to give up the world. If you give a good ringing testimony for the Son of God, the world will give you up pretty quick; they won't want you."

August 24th.

If in this life only we have hope in Christ, we are of all men most miserable.—1 Corinthians xv. 19.

TO deny the resurrection is to say that we will never see more of the loved ones whose bodies have been committed to the clay. If Christ has not risen, this life is the only one, and we are as the brutes.

How cruel it is to have any one love you if this be true ! How horrible that they should let the tendrils of your heart twine around them, if, when they are torn away in death, that is to be the end! I would rather *hate* than *love* if I thought there would be no resurrection, because then I would feel no pangs at losing the hated thing. Oh, the cruelty of unbelief! It takes away our brightest hopes.

AUGUST 25th.

And Samuel said, Hath the Lord as great delight in burnt-offerings and sacrifices, as in obeying the voice of the Lord? Behold, to obey is better than sacrifice, and to hearken than the fat of rams.—1 Samuel xv. 22.

DID you ever notice all but the heart of man obeys God? If you look through history, you will find that this is true. In the beginning God said, " Let there be light," and there was light. " Let the waters bring forth," and the water brought forth abundantly. And one of the proofs that Jesus Christ is God is that He spoke to nature, and nature obeyed Him. At one time He spoke to the sea, and the sea recognized and obeyed. He spoke to the fig-tree, and instantly it withered and died, it obeyed literally and at once. He spoke to devils, and the devils fled. He spoke to the grave, and the grave obeyed Him and gave back its dead. But when He speaks to man, man will not obey Him. That is why man is out of harmony with God, and it will never be different until men learn to obey God. God wants obedience, and He will have it, else there can be no harmony.

August 26th.

In God have I put my trust: I will not be afraid what men can do unto me.—Psalms lvi. 11.

IF God has hid me in the secret pavilion, let men slander me and abuse me if they like! If I can say that God is my Father, Jesus is my Saviour, and heaven is my home: let the world rail, let the flesh do what it pleases, I will not be afraid of evil tidings, for my trust is in God! Is not that a good footing for eternity? "Heaven and earth shall pass away, but My word shall not pass away." If you get your feet fair and square on the rock, let the waves beat if they will. A Christian once said that he trembled sometimes, but the foundation never did: he had his feet upon the rock.

August 27th.

That they should seek the Lord, if haply they might feel after Him, and find Him, though He be not far from every one of us.—Acts xvii. 27.

PHILOSOPHERS are agreed that even the most primitive races of mankind reach out beyond the world of matter to a superior Being. It is as natural for man to feel after God as it is for the ivy to feel after support. Hunger and thirst drive him to seek for food, and there is a hunger of the soul that needs satisfying, too. Man does not need to be commanded to worship, as there is not a race so high or so low in the scale of civilization but has some kind of a god. What man needs is to be directed aright in his worship.

AUGUST 28th.

He shall call upon me, and I will answer Him.— Psalm xci. 15.

LISTEN to the prodigal: "Father, I have sinned!" That was enough; the father took him right to his bosom. The past was blotted out at once.

Look at the men on the day of Pentecost. Their hands were dripping with the blood of the Son of God; they had murdered Jesus Christ. And what did Peter say to them? "It shall come to pass, that whosoever shall call on the name of the Lord shall be saved."

Look at the penitent thief. It might have been that when a little boy, his mother taught him that same passage in Joel, "It shall come to pass, that whosoever shall call on the name of the Lord shall be saved." As he hung there on the cross, it flashed into his mind that this was the Lord of glory, and though he was on the very borders of hell, he cried out, "Lord, remember me," and the answer came right then and there, "This day thou shalt be with Me in paradise." In the morning, as black as hell could make him; in the evening, not a spot or wrinkle. Why? Because he took God at His word. Why will men doubt Him?

AUGUST 29th.

Then touched He their eyes, saying, According to your faith be it unto you.—Matthew ix. 29.

I REMEMBER a man telling me he preached for a number of years without any result. He used to say to his wife as they went to church that he knew the people would not believe anything he said; and there was no blessing. At last he saw his error; he asked God to help him, and took courage, and then the blessing came.

"According to your faith it shall be unto you." This man had expected nothing, and he got just what he expected. Let us expect that God is going to use us. Let us have courage and go forward, looking to God to do great things.

AUGUST 30th.

Think not that I am come to destroy the law, or the prophets: I am not come to destroy, but to fulfill. For verily I say unto you, Till heaven and earth pass, one jot or one tittle shall in no wise pass from the law, till all be fulfilled.—Matthew v. 17, 18.

JESUS never condemned the law and the prophets, but He did condemn those who did not obey them. Because He gave new commandments it does not follow that He abolished the old. Christ's explanation of them made them all the more searching. In His

Sermon on the Mount He carried the principles of the commandments beyond the mere letter. He unfolded them and showed that they embraced more, that they are positive as well as prohibitive. The Old Testament closes with these words:

" Remember ye the law of Moses my servant, which I commanded unto him in Horeb for all Israel, with the statutes and judgments. Behold, I will send you Elijah the prophet before the coming of the great and dreadful day of the Lord: and he shall turn the heart of the fathers to the children, and the heart of the children to their fathers, lest I come and smite the earth with a curse."

Does that look as if the law of Moses was becoming obsolete ?

AUGUST 31st.

These all died in faith, not having received the promises, but having seen them afar off, and were persuaded of them, and embraced them, and confessed that they were strangers and pilgrims on the earth.— Hebrews xi. 13.

WE ought in these days to have far more faith than Abel, or Enoch, or Abraham had. They lived away on the other side of the Cross. We talk about the faith of Elijah, and the patriarchs and prophets; but they lived in the dim light of the past, while we are in the full blaze of Calvary and the resurrection. When we look back and think of what Christ did, how He poured out His blood that men might be saved, we ought to go forth in His strength and conquer the world. Our God is able to do great and mighty things.

SEPTEMBER 1st.

Whosoever therefore shall be ashamed of Me and of My words in this adulterous and sinful generation; of him also shall the Son of man be ashamed, when He cometh in the glory of His Father with the holy angels. —Mark viii. 38.

I DO not believe there is any false religion in the world that men are not proud of. The only religion of which I have ever heard, that men were ashamed of, is the religion of Jesus Christ. I preached two weeks in Salt Lake City, and I did not find a Mormon that was not proud of his religion. When within forty miles of Salt Lake City, the engineer came into the car and wanted to know if I wouldn't like to ride on the engine. I went with him, and in that forty mile ride he talked Mormonism to me the whole time, and tried to convert me so that I would not preach against the Mormons. But how many, many times I have found men ashamed of the religion of Jesus Christ, the only religion that gives men the power over their affections and lusts and sins!

SEPTEMBER 2d.

Son, be of good cheer ; thy sins are forgiven thee.— Matthew ix. 2.

THAT was more than his friends expected; they only thought of his body being made whole. So let us bring our friends to Christ, and we shall get more than we expect.

The Lord met this man's deepest need first. It may be his sins had brought on the palsy, so the Lord forgave the man's sin first of all.

SEPTEMBER 3d.

Joseph of Arimathea, an honorable counsellor, which also waited for the kingdom of God, came, and went in boldly unto Pilate, and craved the body of Jesus.— Mark xv. 43.

I CONSIDER this one of the sublimest, grandest acts that any man ever did. In the darkness and gloom, His disciples having all forsaken Him, Judas having sold Him for thirty pieces of silver, the chief apostle Peter having denied Him with a curse, swearing that he never knew Him, the chief priests having found Him guilty of blasphemy, the council having condemned Him to death, and when there was a hiss going up to heaven from over all Jerusalem, Joseph went right against the current, right against the influence of all his friends, and begged the body of Jesus.

Blessed act! Doubtless he upbraided himself

for not having been more bold in his defence of
Christ when He was tried, and before He was
condemned to be crucified. The Scripture says
he was an honorable man, an honorable coun-
cillor, a rich man, and yet we have only the
record of that one thing—the one act of beg-
ging the body of Jesus. But what he did for
the Son of God, out of pure love for Him, will
live forever; that one act rises up above everything else that Joseph of Arimathea ever did.

SEPTEMBER 4th.

*And he said unto Jesus, Lord, remember me when
Thou comest into Thy kingdom. And Jesus said unto
him, Verily I say unto thee, To-day shalt thou be with
Me in paradise.*—Luke xxiii. 42, 43.

WHEN a prominent man dies, we are anxious to get his last words and acts. The
last act of the Son of God was to save a sinner. That was a part of the glory of His
death. He commenced His ministry by saving
sinners, and ended it by saving this poor thief.

SEPTEMBER 5th.

*Verily, verily, I say unto you, He that believeth on
Me, the works that I do shall he do also ; and greater
works than these shall he do ; because I go unto My
Father.*—John xiv. 12.

I USED to stumble over that verse, but the
longer I live the more I am convinced it is
a greater thing to influence a man whose will is

set against God, to have that will broken and brought into subjection to God's will—or, in other words, it is a greater thing to have power over a living, sinning, God-hating man, than to quicken the dead. He who could create a world could speak a dead man into life; but I think the greatest miracle this world has ever seen was the miracle at Pentecost. The men who surrounded the apostles were full of prejudice, full of malice, full of bitterness, their hands, as it were, dripping with the blood of the Son of God; and yet an unlettered man, a man whom they detested and hated, stood up and preached the gospel, and three thousand of them were immediately convicted and converted, and became disciples of the Lord Jesus Christ.

SEPTEMBER 6th.

If any man be in Christ, he is a new creature : old things are passed away ; behold, all things are become new.—2 Corinthians v. 17.

I SAW an advertisement which read like this : "If you want people to respect you, wear good clothes." That is the world's idea of getting the world's respect. Why! A leper may put on good clothes, but he is a leper still. Mere profession doesn't transform a man. It is the new nature spoken of in Corinthians, "Therefore if any man be in Christ, he is a new creature; old things are passed away; behold, all things are become new."

September 7th.

Work out your own salvation with fear and trembling. For it is God which worketh in you both to will and to do of His good pleasure.—Philippians ii. 12, 13.

I HAVE very little sympathy with any man who has been redeemed by the precious blood of the Son of God, and who has not got the spirit of work. If we are children of God we ought not to have a lazy drop of blood in our veins. If a man tells me that he has been saved, and does not desire to work for the honor of God, I doubt his salvation.

Laziness belongs to the old creation, not to the new. In all my experience I never knew a lazy man to be converted—never. I have more hope for the salvation of drunkards, and thieves, and harlots than of a lazy man.

September 8th.

Jesus answered and said unto him, Verily, verily, I say unto thee, Except a man be born again, he cannot see the kingdom of God.—John iii. 3.

THE only way to get into the kingdom of God is to be " born " into it. The law of this country requires that the President should be born in the country. When foreigners come to our shores they have no right to complain against such a law, which forbids them from ever becoming presidents. Now, has not God a right to make a law that all those who become heirs of eternal life must be " born " into His kingdom ?

An unregenerated man would rather be in hell than in heaven. Take a man whose heart is full of corruption and wickedness, and place him in heaven among the pure, the holy and the redeemed; and he would not want to stay there. Certainly, if we are to be happy in heaven we must begin to make a heaven here on earth. Heaven is a prepared place for a prepared people. If men were taken to heaven just as they are by nature, without having their hearts regenerated, there would be another rebellion in heaven. Heaven is filled with a company of those who have been TWICE BORN.

SEPTEMBER 9th.

Jesus said unto her, I am the resurrection, and the life: he that believeth in Me, though he were dead, yet shall he live.—John xi. 25.

AT the battle of Inkerman a soldier was just able to crawl to his tent after he was struck down. When found, he was lying upon his face, his open Bible before him, his hand glued fast to the page by his life-blood which covered it. When his hand was lifted, the letters of the printed page were clearly traced upon it, and with the ever-living promise in and on his hand, they laid him in a soldier's grave. The words were:

"I am the resurrection and the life; he that believeth in Me, though he were dead, yet shall he live."

I want a religion that can comfort even in death, that can unite me with my loved ones. Oh, what gloom and darkness would settle upon this world if it was not for the glorious doctrine of the resurrection! Thank God, the glorious morning will soon break. For a little while God asks us to be on the watch-tower, faithful to Him and waiting for the summons. Soon our Lord will come to receive His own, whether they be living or dead.

September 10th.

Wherefore putting away lying, speak every man truth with his neighbor: for we are members one of another.—Ephesians iv. 25.

WE have got nowadays so that we divide lies into white lies and black lies, society lies, business lies, and so on. The Word of God knows no such letting-down of the standard. A lie is a lie, no matter what are the circumstances under which it is uttered, or by whom. I have heard that in Siam they sew up the mouth of a confirmed liar. I am afraid if that was the custom in this land, a good many would suffer.

Parents should begin with their children while they are young and teach them to be strictly truthful at all times. There is a proverb: " A lie has no legs." It requires other lies to support it. Tell one lie and you are forced to tell others to back it up.

September 11th.

Enter ye in at the strait gate: for wide is the gate, and broad is the way, that leadeth to destruction, and many there be which go in thereat: because strait is the gate, and narrow is the way, which leadeth unto life, and few there be that find it.—Matthew vii. 13, 14.

MANY a man would be willing to enter into the kingdom of God, if he could do it without giving up sin. People sometimes wonder why Jesus Christ, who lived six hundred years before Mohammed, has got fewer disciples than Mohammed to-day. There is no difficulty in explaining that. A man may become a disciple of Mohammed, and continue to live in the foulest, blackest, deepest sin; but a man cannot be a disciple of Christ without giving up sin.

September 12th.

Withhold not good from them to whom it is due, when it is in the power of thine hand to do it.—Proverbs iii. 27.

AFTER the Chicago fire I came to New York for money, and I heard there was a rich man in Fall River who was very liberal. So I went to him. He gave me a check for a large amount, and then got into his carriage and drove with me to the houses of other rich men in the city, and they all gave me checks. When he left me at the train I grasped his hand and said:

"If you ever come to Chicago, call on me, and I will return your favor."

He said: "Mr. Moody, don't wait for me; do it to the first man that comes along."

I never forget that remark; it had the ring of the true good Samaritan.

SEPTEMBER 13th.

Great peace have they who love Thy law; and nothing shall offend them.—Psalm cxix. 165.

THE study of God's Word will secure peace. Take those Christians who are rooted and grounded in the Word of God, and you will find they have great peace; but it is these who don't study their Bible, who are easily offended when some little trouble comes, or some little persecution. Just a little breath of opposition, and their peace is all gone.

SEPTEMBER 14th.

My son, give Me thine heart, and let thine eyes observe My ways.—Proverbs xxiii. 26.

I REMEMBER hearing a story about an Indian who wanted to come to the Lord. He brought his blanket, but the Lord wouldn't have it. He brought his gun, his dog, his bow and arrow, but the Lord wouldn't have them. At last he brought himself, and the Lord took him. The Lord wanted himself.

What the Lord wants is not what you have got, but yourself, and you cannot do a thing to please God until you surrender yourself to Him.

SEPTEMBER 15th.

Verily, verily, I say unto you, Except a corn of wheat fall into the ground and die, it abideth alone: but if it die, it bringeth forth much fruit.—John xii. 24.

TAKE a little black flower seed and sow it; after it has been planted some time, dig it up. If it is whole you know that it has no life; but if it has begun to decay, you know that life and fruitfulness will follow. There will be a resurrected life, and out of that little black seed will come a beautiful fragrant flower.

Here is a disgusting grub, crawling along the ground. By and by old age overtakes it, and it begins to spin its own shroud, to make its own sepulchre, and it lies as if in death. Look again, and it has shuffled off its shroud, it has burst its sepulchre open, and it comes forth a beautiful butterfly, with different form and habits.

So with our bodies. They die, but God will give us glorified bodies in their stead. This is the law of the new creation as well as of the old: light after darkness: life after death: fruitfulness and glory after corruption and decay.

September 16th.

From above the horse gate repaired the priests, every one over against his house.—Nehemiah iii. 28.

IF this world is going to be reached, I am convinced it must be done by men and women of average talent. After all, there are comparatively few people in the world who have great talents. Here is a man with one talent; there is another with three; perhaps I may have only half a talent. But if we all go to work and trade with the gifts we have, the Lord will prosper us, and we may double or treble our talents. What we need is to be up and about our Master's work, every man building against his own house. The more we use the means and opportunities we have, the more will our ability and our opportunities be increased.

September 17th.

And Simeon blessed them, and said unto Mary His mother, Behold, this child is set for the fall and rising again of many in Israel.—Luke ii. 34.

DO you know that the gospel of Jesus Christ proves either a savor of life unto life, or of death unto death? You sometimes hear people say: "We will go and hear this man preach. If it does us no good, it will do us no harm." Don't you believe it! Every time one hears the gospel and rejects it, the hardening process goes on. The same sun that melts the ice hardens the clay. The sermon that would have moved to action a few years ago makes no impression now.

There is not a true minister of the gospel who will not say that the hardest people to reach are those who have been impressed, and whose impressions have worn away. It is a good deal easier to commit a sin the second time than it was to commit it the first time, but it is a good deal harder to repent the second time than the first.

SEPTEMBER 18th.

And Zacchæus stood, and said unto the Lord, Behold, Lord, the half of my goods I give to the poor; and if I have taken anything from any man by false accusation, I restore him fourfold.—Luke xix. 8.

A SHORT speech; but how the words have come ringing down through the ages!

By making that remark Zacchæus confessed his sin—that he had been dishonest. Besides that, he showed that he knew the requirements of the law of Moses. If a man had taken what did not belong to him, he was not only to return it, but to multiply it by four. I think that men in this dispensation ought to be fully as honest as men under the Law. I am getting so tired and sick of your mere sentimentalism, that does not straighten out a man's life. We may sing our hymns and psalms, and offer prayers, but they will be an abomination to God, unless we are willing to be thoroughly straightforward in our daily life. Nothing will give Christianity such a hold upon the world as to have God's believing people begin to act in this way. Zacchæus had probably more influence in Jericho after he made restitution than any other man in it.

SEPTEMBER 19th.

To him that worketh not, but believeth on him that justifieth the ungodly, his faith is counted for righteousness.—Romans iv. 5.

I FREELY admit salvation is worth working for. It is worth a man's going round the world on his hands and knees, climbing its mountains, crossing its valleys, swimming its rivers, going through all manner of hardship in order to attain it. But we do not get it in that way. It is to him that *believeth.*

SEPTEMBER 20th.

And he saith unto me, Write, Blessed are they which are called unto the marriage supper of the Lamb.—Revelation xix. 9.

I WOULD rather die to-night and be sure of sharing the bliss of the purified in yon world of light than live for centuries with the wealth of this world at my feet, and miss the marriage supper of the Lamb. I have missed many appointments in my life, but by the grace of God I mean to make sure of that one. Why, the blessed privilege of sitting down at the marriage supper of the Lamb, to see the King in His beauty, to be forever with the Lord—who would miss it ?

SEPTEMBER 21st.

As thy days, so shall thy strength be.—Deuteronomy xxxiii. 25.

MANY look forth at the Christian life, and fear that they will not have sufficient strength to hold out to the end. They forget the promise "As thy days, thy strength." It reminds me of the pendulum to the clock which grew disheartened at the thought of having to travel so many thousands of miles ; but when it reflected that the distance was to be accomplished by "tick, tick, tick," it took fresh courage to go its daily journey.

So it is the special privilege of the Christian to commit himself to the keeping of his heavenly Father, and to trust Him day by day. It is a comforting thing to know that the Lord will not begin the good work without also finishing it.

SEPTEMBER 22d.

Wherefore come out from among them, and be ye separate, saith the Lord, and touch not the unclean thing ; and I will receive you.—2 Corinthians vi. 17.

I BELIEVE that a Christian man should lead a separated life. The line between the church and the world is almost obliterated to-day. I have no sympathy with the idea that you must hunt up an old musty church record in order to find out whether a man is a member of the church or not. A man ought to live so that everybody will know he is a Christian. The Bible tells us to lead a separate life. You may lose influence, but you will gain it at the same time. I suppose Daniel was the most unpopular man in Babylon at a certain time, but, thank God, he has outlived all the other men of his day.

September 23d.

Moses My servant is dead; now therefore arise, go over this Jordan, thou, and all this people, unto the land which I do give to them, even to the children of Israel.—Joshua i. 2.

WE need the courage that will compel us to move forward.

We may have to go against the advice of lukewarm Christians; there are some who never seem to do anything but object, because the work is not carried on exactly according to their ideas. They are very fruitful in raising objections to any plans that can be suggested. If any onward step is taken they are ready to throw cold water on it; and suggest all kinds of difficulties. We want to have such faith and courage as shall enable us to move forward without waiting for these timid unbelievers.

SEPTEMBER 24th.

Though I speak with the tongues of men and of angels, and have not love, I am become as sounding brass, or a tinkling cymbal.—1 Corinthians xiii. 1.

IF we want to be wise in winning souls and to be vessels meet for the Master's use, we must get rid of the accursed spirit of self-seeking. That is the meaning of this chapter in Paul's letter. He told the Corinthians that a man might be full of faith and zeal, he might be very benevolent, but if he had not love he was like sounding brass and a tinkling cymbal. I believe many men might as well go into the pulpit and blow a tin horn Sabbath after Sabbath as go on preaching without love. A man may preach the truth; he may be perfectly sound in doctrine; but if there is no love in his heart going out to those whom he addresses, and if he is doing it professionally, the apostle says he is only a sounding brass.

SEPTEMBER 25th.

Verily, verily, I say unto you, He that heareth My word, and believeth on Him that sent Me, hath everlasting life, and shall not come into condemnation; but is passed from death unto life.—John v. 24.

NOTE that the difference between a believer and unbeliever is right here. An unbeliever is living in his day, and he has nothing but a long dark eternal night to look forward to; a Christian is now living in his night, and he has a grand morning that he is looking forward to. The day is ahead, the glory is ahead, the best of life is ahead; it is not behind. That is the teaching of Scripture. For a man whose life is hid with Christ in God, judgment is already passed; he will not come into judgment. Christ was judged for me, and judgment is behind me, not before me.

SEPTEMBER 26th.

I take pleasure in infirmities, in reproaches, in necessities, in persecutions, in distresses for Christ's sake: for when I am weak, then am I strong.—2 Corinthians xii. 10.

THE devil thought he had done a very wise thing when he got Paul into prison, but he was very much mistaken; he overdid it for once. I have no doubt Paul has thanked God ever since for that Philippian jail, and for his stripes and imprisonment there. The world has made more by it than we shall ever know till we get to heaven.

SEPTEMBER 27th.

The way of transgressors is hard.—Proverbs xiii. 15.

DO you mean to say that God is a hard master? that it is a hard thing to serve God, that Satan is an easy master, and that it is easier to serve him than God? God a hard maste ' 'f I read my Bible right, I read *that the way of transgressors is hard.* It is the devil who is the hard master. If you doubt it, young man, look at the convict in the prison, right in the bloom of manhood, right in the prime of life. He has been there for ten years, and must remain for ten years more—twenty years taken out of his life; and when he comes out of that miserable cell, he comes out a branded felon! Do you think *that* man will tell you that the way of the transgressor has been easy?

Go ask the poor drunkard, the man who is bound hand and foot, the slave of the infernal cup, who is hastening onward to a drunkard's hell. Ask him if he has found the way of the transgressor easy. "Easy?" he will cry; "easy? The way of the transgressor is hard, and gets harder and harder every day!"

Go ask the libertine and the worldling, go ask the gambler and the blasphemer, take the most faithful follower of the devil and put the questions to him; with one voice they will all tell you that the service has been hard.

SEPTEMBER 28th.

Then said they unto Him, Lord, evermore give us this bread.—John vi. 34.

I CANNOT but believe that the reason for the standard of Christian life being so low, is that we are living on stale manna. You know what I mean by that. So many people are living on their past experience—thinking of the grand times they had twenty years ago, perhaps when they were converted. It is a sure sign that we are out of communion with God if we are talking more of the joy and peace and power we had in the past, than of what we have to-day. We are told to "grow in grace"; but a great many are growing the wrong way. The Israelites used to gather the manna fresh every day: they were not allowed to store it up. There is a lesson here for us. If we would be strong and vigorous, we must go to God daily. A man can no more take in a supply of grace for the future than he can eat enough to-day to last him for the next six months, or take sufficient air into his lungs at once to sustain life for a week to come. We must draw upon God's boundless stores of grace from day to day, as we need it.

September 29th.

And not many days after the younger son gathered all together, and took his journey into a far country, and there wasted his substance with riotous living.—Luke xv. 13.

HE started off, holding his head very high that morning. He was full of pride and conceit, and he had very lofty ideas. If any one had told him what he was coming to, he would have laughed in scorn. But mind you, once a man starts on the downward track, he will sink lower and lower, unless by the grace of God he turns from sin to righteousness. The first lie, the first drink, the first petty theft, is often a crisis in a man's life.

SEPTEMBER 30th.

And the lord said unto the servant, Go out into the highways and hedges, and compel them to come in, that my house may be filled.—Luke xiv. 23.

IS it not time for us to launch out into the deep? I have never seen people go out into the lanes and alleys, into the hedges and highways, and try to bring the people in, but the Lord gave His blessing. If a man has the courage to go right to his neighbor and speak to him about his soul, God is sure to smile upon the effort. The person who is spoken to may wake up cross, but that is not always a bad sign, he may write a letter next day and apologize. At any rate it is better to wake him up in this way than that he should continue to slumber on to death and ruin.

OCTOBER 1st.

God commendeth His love toward us, in that, while we were yet sinners, Christ died for us.—Romans v. 8.

I KNOW of no truth in the whole Bible that ought to come home to us with such power and tenderness as that of the Love of God.

There is no truth in the Bible that Satan would so much like to blot out. For more than six thousand years he has been trying to persuade men that God does not love them. He succeeded in making our first parents believe this lie; and too often he succeeds with their children.

The idea that God does not love us often comes from false teaching. Mothers make a mistake in teaching children that God does not love them when they do wrong, but only when they do right. That is not taught in Scripture. *You* do not teach your children that when they do wrong you hate them. Their wrongdoing does not change your love to hate; if it did, you would change your love a great many times. Because your child is fretful, or has committed some act of disobedience, you do not cast him out as though he did not belong to you! No! he is still your child; and you love him. And if men have gone astray from God it does not follow that He hates *them*. It is the sin that He hates.

OCTOBER 2d.

Trust in Him at all times ye people.—Psalm lxii. 8.

THERE are a good many who trust God when they see all is light and clear before them, but not in the dark. They will trust when everything is fair and bright—no opposition, no persecution or bitterness, but all smooth sailing. Well, that is walking by sight, and not by faith. We are to trust in the Lord at all times. The Lord will not have one who cannot be tried. If you are starting out in the Lord's work, you are going to be tempted. St. Augustine said that God has had one Son without sin, but no son without trial.

OCTOBER 3d.

All these blessings shall come on thee, and overtake thee, if thou shalt hearken unto the voice of the Lord thy God.—Deuteronomy xxviii. 2.

DO you know *every man who was blessed while Christ was on earth, was blessed in the act of obedience?*

Ten lepers came to Him, and He said, "Go and show yourselves to the priest." They might have said, "What good is that going to do us? It was the priest that sent us away from our families." But they said nothing; and it came to pass, that, as they went, they were healed. Do you want to get rid of the leprosy of sin? Obey God. You say you don't feel like it. Did you always feel like going to school when you were a boy? Supposing a man only went to business when he felt like it; he would fail in a few weeks.

Jesus said to another man, "Go to the Pool of Siloam and wash," and as he washed, he received his sight. He was blessed in the act of obedience.

The prophet said to Naaman, "Go and dip seven times in Jordan," and while he was dipping he was healed. Simple obedience.

OCTOBER 4th.

For whether we be beside ourselves, it is to God: or whether we be sober, it is for your cause.—2 Corinthians v. 13.

IN my opinion no one is fit for God's service until he is willing to be considered mad by the world. They said Paul was mad. I wish we had many more who were bitten with the same kind of madness. As some one has said: "If we are mad, we have a good Keeper on the way and a good Asylum at the end of the road."

OCTOBER 5th.

And as they came down from the mountain, He charged them that they should tell no man what things they had seen, till the Son of man were risen from the dead.—Mark ix. 9.

IT is a singular fact that John, the only one of the four evangelists that was with Christ on the Mount of Transfiguration, is the only one who does not give an account of it. Perhaps the scene was so solemn, so impressive, and so holy that he could not bring himself to write of it. Peter, who was also present, barely mentioned it in his writings that have come down to us. His only reference to the scene is in his second epistle, written many years afterward, when he was an old man:

"We were eyewitnesses of His majesty; for He received from God the Father honor and glory, when there came such a voice to Him from the excellent glory, This is My beloved Son, in whom I am well pleased. And this voice, which came from heaven, we heard when we were with Him in the holy mount."

OCTOBER 6th.

And ye will not come to Me, that ye might have life. —John v. 40.

THE battle is fought on that one word of the will; the door hangs on that one hinge of the will. Will you obey? That is the question! Will you obey the voice of God and do as He commands you? No man can obey for you any more than he can eat and drink for you. You must eat and drink for yourself, and you must obey God for yourself.

OCTOBER 7th.

Because he hath set his love upon Me, therefore will I deliver him.—Psalm xci. 14.

WE all have some weak point in our charac- ter. When we would go forward, it drags us back, and when we would rise up into higher spheres of usefulness and the atmosphere of heaven, something drags us down. Now I have no sympathy with the idea that God puts us behind the blood and saves us, and then leaves us in Egypt to be under the old taskmaster. I believe God brings us out of Egypt into the promised land, and that it is the privilege of every child of God to be delivered from every foe, from every besetting sin.

If there is some sin that is getting the mastery over you, you certainly cannot be useful. You certainly cannot bring forth fruit to the honor and glory of God until you get self-control.

OCTOBER 8th.

Behold, God is my salvation; I will trust, and not be afraid: for the Lord Jehovah is my strength and my song; He also is become my salvation.—Isaiah xii. 2.

DON'T be watching your feelings. There is not one verse from Genesis to Revelation about being saved by feeling. When the devil sees a poor soul in agony in the waves of sin, and getting close to the Rock of Ages, he just holds out the plank of "feeling" to him, and says,

"There, get on that; you feel more comfortable now, don't you?"

And while the man is getting his breath again, out goes the plank from under him, and he is worse off than ever. Accept no refuge but the Rock,—the Everlasting Strength.

OCTOBER 9th.

He that overcometh shall inherit all things; and I will be his God and he shall be My son.—Revelation xxi. 7.

AFTER the Chicago fire I met a man who said,

"Moody, I hear you lost everything in the Chicago fire."

"Well," I said, "you understood it wrong; I didn't."

He said, "How much have you left?"

"I can't tell you; I have got a good deal more left than I lost."

"You can't tell how much you have?"

"No."

"I didn't know that you were ever that rich. What do you mean?"

"I mean just what I say. I got my old Bible out of the fire; that is about the only thing. One promise came to me that illuminated the city a great deal more than the fire did. 'He that overcometh shall inherit all things; and I will be his God and he shall be My son.'"

You ask me how much I am worth. I don't know. You may go and find out how much the Vanderbilts are worth, and the Astors, and Rothschilds, but you can't find out how much a child of God is worth. Why? Because he is a joint-heir with Jesus Christ.

Why are you going around with your head down, talking about your poverty? The weakest, poorest child of God is richer than a Vanderbilt, because he has eternal riches. The stuff that burned up in Chicago was like the dust in the balance. Joint-heir with Jesus Christ! That is what the eighth of Romans teaches us.

OCTOBER 10th.

He must increase, but I must decrease.—John iii. 30.

IF we preached down ourselves and exalted Christ, the world would soon be reached. The world is perishing to-day for the want of Christ. The church could do without our theories and pet views, but not without Christ; and when her ministers get behind the cross, so that Christ is held up, the people will come flocking to hear the gospel.

Selfishness is one of the greatest hindrances to the cause of Christ. Every one wants the chief seat in the synagogue. One prides himself that he is pastor of this church, and another of that. Would to God we could get all this out of the way, and say, "He must increase, but I must decrease." We cannot do it, however, except we get down at the foot of the cross. Human nature likes to be lifted up; the grace of God alone can humble us.

October 11th.

Bring forth therefore fruits meet for repentance.—
Matthew iii. 8.

A FRIEND had come to Christ and wished
to consecrate himself and his wealth to
God. He had formerly had transactions with
the government, and had taken advantage of
them. This thing came up when he was converted, and his conscience troubled him. He
said,

"I want to consecrate my wealth, but it
seems as if God will not take it."

He had a terrible struggle; his conscience
kept rising up and smiting him. At last he
drew a check for fifteen hundred dollars and sent
it to the United States Treasury. He told me
he received such a blessing when he had done it!

That was bringing forth "fruits meet for repentance." I believe a great many men are
crying to God for light, and they are not getting
it because they are not honest with themselves.

October 12th.

I will show him My salvation.—Psalm xci. 16.

I BELIEVE we don't learn the fringe of the
subject of salvation down here. When our
Master was on earth, He said He had many
more things to say, but He could not reveal
them to His disciples because they were not

ready to receive them. But when we go yonder, where these mortal bodies have put on immortality, when our spiritual faculties are loosed from the thralldom of the flesh, I believe we shall be able to take more in. God will lead us from glory to glory, and show us the fullness of our salvation. Don't you think Moses knew more at the Mount of Transfiguration than he did at Pisgah? Didn't Christ talk with him then about the death He was to accomplish at Jerusalem? He couldn't have received this truth before, any more than the disciples, but when he had received his glorified body, Christ could show him everything.

OCTOBER 13th.

Honor thy father and mother; which is the first commandment with promise; that it may be well with thee, and thou mayest live long on the earth.—Ephesians vi. 23.

DISOBEDIENCE and disrespect for parents are often the first steps in the downward track. Many a criminal has testified that these are the points where he first went astray. I have lived over sixty years, and I have learned one thing if I have learned nothing else—that no man or woman who dishonors father or mother ever prospers, in the long run.

October 14th.

And the Lord said, Simon, Simon, behold, Satan hath desired to have you, that he may sift you as wheat: but I have prayed for thee, that thy faith fail not: and when thou art converted, strengthen thy brethren. —Luke xxii. 31, 32.

THERE is no one beyond the reach of the tempter. Keep that in mind. Life may run smoothly for a while, but the testing time is coming.

October 15th.

Peter said, Ananias, why hath Satan filled thine heart to lie . . . ?—Acts v. 3.

"MR. MOODY," you say, "how can I check myself? how can I overcome the habit of lying and gossip?" A lady once said to me that she had got so into the habit of exaggerating that her friends said they could never understand her.

The cure is simple, but not very pleasant. Treat it as a *sin*, and confess it to God and the person whom you have wronged. As soon as you catch yourself lying, go straight to that person and confess you have lied. Let your confession be as wide as your transgression. If you have slandered or lied about any one in public, let your confession be public. Many a person says some mean, false thing about another in the presence of others, and then tries to patch it up by going to that person alone. This is not making adequate confession. I need not go to God with confession until I have made it right with that person, if it is in my power to do so; He will not hear me.

OCTOBER 16th.

He that dwelleth in the secret place of the most High shall abide under the shadow of the Almighty.—Psalm xci. 1.

THE psalm might have been written by Moses after some terrible calamity had come upon the children of Israel. It might have been after that terrible night of death in Egypt, when the firstborn from the palace to the hovel were slain; or after that terrible plague of fiery serpents in the wilderness, when the people were full of fear and in a nervous state. Perhaps Moses called Aaron and Miriam, and Joshua and Caleb, and a few others into his tent and read this psalm to them first. How sweet it must have sounded, and how strange!

I can imagine Moses asking, " Do you think that will help them? Will that quiet them?" and they all thought that it would. And then, (it may be), on one of those hilltops of Sinai, at twilight, this psalm was read. How it must have soothed them, how it must have helped them, how it must have strengthened them!

October 17th.

Grow in grace, and in the knowledge of our Lord and Saviour Jesus Christ.—2 Peter iii. 18.

ALTHOUGH you may be born again, it will require time to become a full-grown Christian. Justification is instantaneous, but sanctification is a life-work. We are to grow in wisdom. We are to add grace to grace. A tree may be perfect in its first year of growth, but it has not attained its maturity. So with the Christian: he may be a true child of God, but not a matured Christian.

October 18th.

Then went out to him Jerusalem, and all Judæa, and all the region around about Jordan, and were baptized of him in Jordan, confessing their sins.—Matthew iii. 5, 6.

THINK of the whole population going out into the wilderness to hear this wonderful open-air preacher, to be " baptized of him in Jordan, confessing their sins!" John was a preacher of *repentance*. Perhaps no one ever rang out the word "Repent!" like John the Baptist. Day after day, as he came out of the desert and stood on the banks of that famous river, you could hear his voice, "Repent! for the kingdom of heaven is at hand." We can almost now hear the echoes of his voice as they floated up and down the Jordan.

Many wonderful scenes had been witnessed at that stream. Naaman had washed away his leprosy there. Elijah and Elisha had crossed it dryshod. Joshua had led through its channel the mighty host of the redeemed on their journey from Egypt into the promised land. But it had never seen anything like this: men, women, and children, mothers with babes in their arms, scribes, Pharisees, Sadducees, publicans and soldiers, flocked from Judea, Samaria and Galilee, to hear this lonely wilderness prophet.

October 19th.

My God shall supply all your need according to His riches in glory by Christ Jesus.—Philippians iv. 19.

LOOK at these words carefully. It does not say He will supply our *wants*. There are many things we want that God has not promised to give. It is our *need*, and *all* our need.

My children often want many things they do not get; but I supply all they need, if it is in my power to do it. I do not supply all their wants by any means. And so, though God may withhold from us many things that we desire, He will supply all our need. There can come upon us no trouble or trial in this life, but God has grace enough to carry us right through it, if we will only go to Him and get it. But we must ask for it day by day. " As thy days, so shall thy strength be."

OCTOBER 20th.

Ho, every one that thirsteth, come ye to the waters, and he that hath no money; come ye, buy, and eat; yea, come, buy wine and milk without money and without price.—Isaiah lv. 1.

I PITY those people who are all the time looking to see what they will have to give up. God wants to bestow His marvellous grace on His people; and there is not a soul who has believed on Jesus, for whom God has not abundance of grace in store.

What would you say of a man dying of thirst on the banks of a beautiful river, with the stream flowing past his feet? You would think he was mad! The river of God's grace flows on without ceasing; why should we not partake of it, and go on our way rejoicing?

OCTOBER 21st.

And suddenly there was with the angel a multitude of the heavenly host praising God, and saying, Glory to God in the highest, and on earth peace, good will toward men.—Luke ii. 13, 14.

I HAVE read that on the shores of the Adriatic sea the wives of fishermen, whose husbands have gone far out upon the deep, are in the habit of going down to the seashore at night and singing the first verse of some beautiful hymn. After they have sung it they listen until they hear brought on the wind across the sea the second verse sung by their brave husbands—and both are happy. Perhaps, if we would listen, we too might hear on this storm-tossed world of ours, some sound, some whisper, borne from afar to tell us there is a heaven which is our home; and when we sing our hymns upon the shores of the earth, perhaps we may hear their sweet echoes breaking in music upon the sands of time, and cheering the hearts of those who are pilgrims and strangers along the way.

OCTOBER 22d.

Whosoever shall keep the whole law, and yet offend in one point, he is guilty of all.—James ii. 10.

THE ten commandments are not ten different laws; they are one law. If I am being held up in the air by a chain with ten links and I break one of them, down I come, just as surely as if I break the whole ten. If I am forbidden to go out of an enclosure, it makes no difference at what point I break through the fence. "Whosoever shall keep the whole law and yet offend in one point, he is guilty of all." "The golden chain of obedience is broken if one link is missing."

OCTOBER 23d.

The fruit of the righteous is a tree of life; and he that winneth souls is wise.—Proverbs xi. 30.

IF we have known Jesus Christ for years, and have not been able to introduce an anxious soul to Him, there has been something wrong somewhere. If we were full of grace, we should be ready for any call that comes to us. Paul said, when he had that famous interview with Christ on the way to Damascus, " Lord, what wilt Thou have me to do? " Isaiah said, " Here am I, send me." No man can tell what he can do until he moves forward. If we do that in the name of God, instead of there being a few scores or hundreds converted, there will be thousands flocking into the Kingdom of God. Remember that we honor God when we ask for great things. It is a humiliating thing to think that we are satisfied with very small results.

OCTOBER 24th.

Be clothed with humility.—1 Peter v. 5.

SOME years ago I saw what is called a sensitive plant. I happened to breathe on it, and suddenly it drooped its head; I touched it, and it withered away. Humility is as sensitive as that; it cannot safely be brought out on exhibition. A man who is flattering himself that he is humble and is walking close to the Master, is self-deceived. Humility consists not in thinking meanly of ourselves, but in not thinking of ourselves at all. Moses wist not that his face shone. If humility speaks of itself, it is gone.

OCTOBER 25th.

O Lord, I beseech thee, let now Thine ear be atten-
tive to the prayer of Thy servant, and to the prayer of
Thy servants, who desire to fear Thy name: and
prosper, I pray thee, Thy servant this day, and grant
him mercy in the sight of this man.—Nehemiah i. 11.

WHEN Nehemiah began to pray I have no
idea that he thought he himself was to
be the instrument in God's hand of building
the walls of Jerusalem. But when a man gets
into sympathy and harmony with God, then
God prepares him for the work He has for him.
No doubt he thought the Persian king might
send one of his great warriors and accomplish
the work with a great army of men; but after
he had been praying for months, it may be, the
thought flashed into his mind:

"Why should not I go to Jerusalem myself
and build those walls?"

Prayer for the work will soon arouse your
own sympathy and effort.

OCTOBER 26th.

And He said unto me, My grace is sufficient for thee;
for My strength is made perfect in weakness. Most
gladly therefore will I rather glory in my infirmities,
that the power of Christ may rest upon me.—1
Corinthians xii. 9.

I FIND that many Christians are in trouble
about the future; they think they will not
have grace enough to die by. It is much more

important that we should have grace enough to live by. It seems to me that death is of very little importance in the meantime. When the dying hour comes there will be dying grace; but you do not require dying grace to live by. If I am going to live for fifteen or twenty years, what do I want with dying grace? I am far more anxious about having grace enough for my present work.

I have sometimes been asked if I had grace enough to enable me to go to the stake and die as a martyr. No; what do I want with martyrs' grace? I do not like suffering; but if God should call on me to die a martyr's death, He would give me martyrs' grace. If I have to pass through some great affliction, I know God will give me grace when the time comes; but I do not want it till it comes.

OCTOBER 27th.

In the last day, that great day of the feast, Jesus stood and cried, saying, If any man thirst, let him come unto Me, and drink.—John vii. 37.

HOW this world is thirsting for something that will satisfy! What fills the places of amusement, the dance houses, the music halls, and the theatres, night after night? Men and women are thirsting for something they have not got. The moment a man turns his back upon God, he begins to thirst; and that thirst will never be quenched until he returns to "the fountain of living waters." As the prophet Jeremiah tells us, we have forsaken the fountain of living waters, and hewn out for ourselves cisterns, broken cisterns, that can hold no water. There is a thirst this world can never quench: the more we drink of its pleasures, the thirstier we become. We cry out for more and more, and we are all the while being dragged down lower and lower. But there is a fountain opened to the House of David for sin and for uncleanness. Let us press up to it, and drink and live.

OCTOBER 28th.

Jesus answered and said unto him, Verily, verily, I say unto thee, Except a man be born again, he cannot see the kingdom of God.—John iii. 3.

IF the words of this text are true they embody one of the most solemn questions. We can afford to be deceived about many things rather than about this one thing. Christ makes it very plain. He says, " Except a man be born again, he cannot *see* the kingdom of God "—much less inherit it.

This doctrine of the new birth is therefore the foundation of all our hopes for the world to come. It is really the A B C of the Christian religion. My experience has been this—that if a man is unsound on this doctrine he will be unsound on almost every other fundamental doctrine in the Bible. A true understanding of this subject will help a man to solve a thousand difficulties that he may meet with in the Word of God. Things that before seemed very dark and mysterious will become very plain.

OCTOBER 29th.

And I heard a voice from heaven saying unto me, Write, Blessed are the dead which die in the Lord from henceforth: Yea, saith the Spirit, that they may rest from their labors; and their works do follow them.— Revelation xiv. 13.

THINK of Paul up yonder. People are going up every day and every hour, men and women who have been brought to Christ through his writings. He set streams in motion that have flowed on for more than a thousand years. I can imagine men going up to him and saying, " Paul, I thank you for writing that letter to the Ephesians; I found Christ in that." " Paul, I thank you for writing that epistle to the Corinthians." " Paul, I found Christ in that epistle to the Philippians." " I thank you, Paul, for that epistle to the Galatians; I found Christ in that."

When Paul was put in prison he did not fold his hands and sit down in idleness! No, he began to write; and his epistles have come down through the ages and brought thousands on thousands to a knowledge of Christ crucified.

October 30th.

And they heard the voice of the Lord God walking in the garden in the cool of the day: and Adam and his wife hid themselves from the presence of the Lord God amongst the trees of the garden.—Genesis iii. 8.

A RULE I have had for years is to treat the Lord Jesus Christ as a personal friend. It is not a creed, a mere empty doctrine, but it is Christ Himself we have. The moment we receive Christ we should receive Him as a friend. When I go away from home I bid my wife and children good-bye, I bid my friends and acquaintances good-bye; but I never heard of a poor backslider going down on his knees and saying:

"I have been near You for ten years. Your service has become tedious and monotonous. I have come to bid You farewell. Good-bye, Lord Jesus Christ!"

I never heard of one doing this. I will tell you how they go away; they just run away.

October 31st.

And from thence, when the brethren heard of us, they came to meet us as far as Appii Forum, and the Three Taverns: whom when Paul saw, he thanked God, and took courage.—Acts xxviii. 15.

IF you are not able to go and invite the people to hear the gospel, you can give a word of cheer to others, and wish them Godspeed.

Many a time when I have come down from the pulpit, some old man, trembling on the very verge of another world, living perhaps on borrowed time, has caught hold of my hand, and in a quavering voice said,

" God bless you ! "

How the words have cheered and helped me ! You can speak a word of encouragement to younger friends, if you are too feeble to work yourselves.

NOVEMBER 1st.

The commandment, which was ordained to life, I found to be unto death. For sin, taking occasion by the commandment, deceived me, and by it slew me.— Romans vii. 10, 11.

A FRIEND in England was telling me that an acquaintance of his, a minister, was once called upon to officiate at a funeral, in the place of a chaplain of one of Her Majesty's prisons, who was absent. He noticed that only one solitary man followed the body of the criminal to the grave. When the grave had been covered, this man told the minister that he was an officer of the law whose duty it was to watch the body of the culprit until it was buried out of sight; that was " the end " of the British law.

And that is what the law of God does to the sinner; it brings him right to death, and leaves him there. I pity deep down in my heart those who are trying to save themselves by the law. It never has, it never will, and it never can save the soul.

NOVEMBER 2d.

Christ is all, and in all.—Colossians iii. 11.

CHRIST is all to us that we make Him to be. I want to emphasize that word "ALL." Some men make Him to be "a root out of a dry ground," "without form or comeliness." He is nothing to them; they do not want Him. Some Christians have a very small Saviour, for they are not willing to receive Him fully, and let Him do great and mighty things for them. Others have a mighty Saviour, because they make Him to be great and mighty.

NOVEMBER 3d.

His divine power hath given unto us all things that pertain unto life and godliness, through the knowledge of Him that hath called us to glory and virtue.—2 Peter i. 3.

THERE is GLORY for the time to come. A great many people seem to forget that the best is before us. Dr. Bonar once said that everything before the true believer is "glorious." This thought took hold on my soul, and I began to look the matter up, and see what I could find in Scripture that was glorious hereafter. I found that the kingdom we are going to inherit is glo-

rious; our crown is to be a " crown of glory ";
the city we are going to inhabit is the city of
the glorified; the songs we are to sing are the
songs of the glorified; we are to wear garments
of " glory and beauty "; our society will be the
society of the glorified; our rest is to be " glorious "; the country to which we are going is to
be full of " the glory of God and of the Lamb."

There are many who are always looking on
the backward path, and mourning over the
troubles through which they have passed; they
keep lugging up the cares and anxieties they
have been called on to bear, and are forever
looking at them. Why should we go reeling
and staggering under the burdens and cares of
life when we have such glorious prospects before us?

NOVEMBER 4th.

Be not faithless, but believing.—John xx. 27.

PEOPLE say, "If I could only get rid of
these doubts and fears, I think I would be
ready to work."

Go to work, and these doubts will disappear.
There is work to be done. Life is short at the
longest, so let us be about our Master's business. While you are engaged in His work,
these doubts will not assail you so much. I believe any Christian would have doubts in less
than six months if he did nothing.

November 5th.

But foolish and unlearned questions avoid, knowing that they do gender strifes.—2 Timothy ii. 23.

THERE are two kinds of sceptics—one class with honest difficulties, and another class who delight only in discussion. I used to think that this latter class would always be a thorn in my flesh, but they do not prick me now. I expect to find them right along the journey. Men of this stamp used to hang around Christ to entangle Him in His talk.

Many young converts make a woful mistake. They think they are to defend the whole Bible. I knew very little of the Bible when I was first converted, and I thought that I had to defend it from beginning to end against all comers. A Boston infidel got hold of me, floored all my arguments at once, and discouraged me. But I have got over that now. There are many things in the Word of God that I do not profess to understand.

November 6th.

We must all appear before the judgment seat of Christ; that every one may receive the things done in his body, according to that he hath done, whether it be good or bad.—2 Corinthians v. 10.

SOME people say that you never can tell till you are before the throne of Judgment whether you are saved or not. Why, if our life is hid with

Christ in God, we are not coming into judgment for our sins. We may come into judgment for *reward*. This is clearly taught where the lord reckoned with the servant to whom five talents had been given, and who brought other five talents. His lord said unto him, " Well done thou good and faithful servant: thou hast been faithful over a few things; I will make thee ruler over many things; enter thou into the joy of thy lord." (Matt. xxv. 20, 21.) We shall be judged for our stewardship—that is one thing; but salvation—eternal life—is quite another thing.

November 7th.

Now the God of hope fill you with all joy and peace in believing, that you may abound in hope through the power of the Holy Ghost.—Romans xv. 13.

NO man or woman is ever used by God to build up His kingdom who has lost hope. Wherever I have found a worker in God's vineyard who has lost hope, I have found a man or woman not very useful.

It is very important to have hope in the church; and it is the work of the Holy Ghost to impart hope. Let Him come into some of the churches where there have not been any conversions for a few years, and let Him convert a score of people, and see how hopeful the church becomes at once. He imparts hope. A man filled with the Spirit of God will be very hopeful. He will be looking out into the future, and he knows that it is all bright, because the God of all grace is able to do great things.

November 8th.

Pray for us: for we trust we have a good conscience, in all things willing to live honestly.—Hebrews xiii. 18.

IS not conscience a safe guide? No, is not. Some people don't seem to have any conscience, and don't know what it means. Their education has a good deal to do with conscience. There are persons who will say that their conscience did not tell them that they had done wrong until after the wrong was done. What we want, is something to tell us a thing is wrong before we do it.

November 9th.

There is no fear in love; but perfect love casteth out fear: because fear hath torment. He that feareth is not made perfect in love.—1 John iv. 18.

THERE cannot be true peace where there is fear. " Perfect love casteth out fear." How wretched a wife would be if she doubted her husband! and how miserable a mother would feel if after her boy had gone away from home she had reason, from his neglect, to question that son's devotion! True love never has a doubt.

November 10th.

What if some did not believe? shall their unbelief make the faith of God without effect?—Romans iii. 3.

I AM so tired of the Christianity that is made up of negations, what people *don't* believe. I met a man some time ago, and he said, " I don't believe this." I talked with him a little, and made another statement; he didn't believe that. Finally, I said, " Man, will you tell me what you do believe?" and I found he didn't believe anything except that he didn't believe.

November 11th.

Ye are the light of the world. A city that is set on an hill cannot be hid.—Matthew v. 14.

GOD has left us down here to shine. We are not here to buy and sell and get gain, to accumulate wealth, to acquire worldly position. This earth, if we are Christians, is not our home; it is yonder. God has sent us into the world to shine for Him—to light up this dark world. Christ came to be the Light of the world, but men put out that light. They took it to Calvary, and blew it out. Before Christ went up on high, He said to His disciples: "Ye are the light of the world. Ye are My witnesses. Go forth and carry the gospel to the perishing nations of the earth."

November 12th.

When He is come, He will reprove the world of sin . . . because they believe not on Me.—John xvi. 8, 9.

SOME men seem to think it is a great misfortune that they do not have faith. They seem to look upon it as a kind of infirmity, and they think they ought to be sympathized with and pitied. Bear in mind it is not a misfortune; it is the most damning sin of the world.

The greatest enemy God and man have got is unbelief. Christ found it on both sides of the cross. It was the very thing that put Him to death. The Jews did not believe Him. They did not believe God had sent Him. They took Him to Calvary and murdered Him. And the first thing we find after He rose from the grave was unbelief again. Thomas, one of His own disciples, did not believe He had risen. He said, "Thomas, feel these wounds;" and Thomas believed, and said, "My Lord and my God."

November 13th.

Neither is there salvation in any other: for there is none other name under heaven given among men, whereby we must be saved.—Acts iv. 12.

IF there is one word above another that will swing open the eternal gates, it is the name of Jesus. There are a great many passwords and bywords down here, but that will be the countersign up above. Jesus Christ is the "Open Sesame" to heaven. Any one who tries to climb up some other way, is a thief and a robber. And when we get in, what a joy above every other joy we can think of, will it be to see Jesus Himself, and to be with Him continually !

NOVEMBER 14th.

Verily, verily, I say unto you, He that heareth My word, and believeth on Him that sent Me, hath everlasting life, and shall not come into condemnation; but is passed from death unto life.—John v. 24.

THE cross of Christ divides all mankind. There are only two sides, those for Christ, and those against Him. Think of the two thieves; from the side of Christ one went down to death cursing God, and the other went to glory.

What a contrast! In the morning he is led out, a condemned criminal; in the evening he is saved from his sins. In the morning he is cursing—Matthew and Mark both tell us that those two thieves came out cursing, in the evening he is singing hallelujahs with a choir of angels. In the morning he is condemned by men as not fit to live on earth; in the evening he is reckoned good enough for heaven. In the morning nailed to the cross; in the evening in the Paradise of God, crowned with a crown he should wear through all the ages. In the morning not an eye to pity; in the evening washed and made clean in the blood of the Lamb. In the morning in the society of thieves and outcasts; in the evening Christ is not ashamed to walk arm-in-arm with him down the golden pavements of the eternal city.

NOVEMBER 15th.

Whom God hath raised up, having loosed the pains of death: because it was not possible that He should be holden of it.—Acts iii. 24.

IT has always been a mystery to me when every disciple of Jesus Christ who was anywhere near Jerusalem, was not at the sepulchre on the morning of the third day after the crucifixion. Over and over again He told them that He would arise. One of the last things He said to them, as they were on their way to the Mount of Olives, was—"After that I am risen, I will go before you into Galilee." But there is not one solitary passage that tells us that they had any expectation of His resurrection. It seems as if His enemies had better memories than His friends. When His body was laid away in the tomb, the Jews went to Pilate, and wanted him to make it secure; because, they said, " We remember that that deceiver said, while He was yet alive, After three days I will rise again."

November 16th.

By grace are ye saved through faith; and that not of yourselves: it is the gift of God: not of works, lest any man should boast.—Ephesians ii. 8, 9.

BEFORE my conversion, I worked toward the cross, but since then I have worked from the cross. Then I worked to be saved; now I work because I am saved.

November 17th.

For John had said unto Herod, It is not lawful for thee to have thy brother's wife.—Mark vi. 18.

IF your minister comes to you frankly, tells you of your sin, and warns you faithfully, thank God for him. He is your best friend; he is a heaven-sent man. But if your minister speaks smooth, oily words to you, tells you it is all right, when you know, and he knows, that it is all wrong, and that you are living in sin, you may be sure that he is a devil-sent man. I want to say I have a contempt for a preacher that will tone his message down to suit some one in his audience; some senator, or big man whom he sees present. If the devil can get possession of such a minister and speak through him, he will do the work better than the devil himself. All the priests and ministers of all the churches cannot save one soul that will not part with sin.

November 18th.

I have fed you with milk, and not with meat: for hitherto ye were not able to bear it, neither yet now are ye able.—1 Corinthians iii. 2.

YOU know it is always regarded a great event in the family when a child can feed itself. It is propped up at table, and at first perhaps it uses the spoon upside down, but by and by it uses it all right, and mother, or perhaps sister, claps her hands and says :

" Just see, baby's feeding himself ! "

What we need as Christians is to be able to feed ourselves. How many there are who sit helpless and listless, with open mouths, hungry for spiritual things, and the minister has to try to feed them, while the Bible is a feast prepared, into which they never venture !

November 19th.

Thou shalt not bear false witness against thy neighbor.—Exodus xx. 16.

YOU don't like to have any one bear false witness against you, or help to ruin your character or reputation ; then why should you do it to others ? How public men are slandered in this country ! None escape, whether good or bad. Judgment is passed upon them, their family, their character, by the press and by individuals who know little or nothing about them.

If one-tenth that is said and written about our public men was true, half of them should be hung. Slander has been called "tongue murder." Slanderers are compared to flies that always settle on sores, but do not touch a man's healthy parts.

If the archangel Gabriel should come down to earth and mix in human affairs, I believe his character would be assailed inside of forty-eight hours. Slander called Christ a gluttonous man and a winebibber. He claimed to be the Truth, but instead of worshipping Him, men took Him and crucified Him.

November 20th.

Who shall lay anything to the charge of God's elect ? It is God that justifieth.—Romans viii. 33.

THAT word "justifieth" seems too good to be true. No wonder that Martin Luther shook all Germany when that truth dawned upon him, "the just shall live by faith." Do you know what "justified" means? I will tell you. It is to stand before God without spot or wrinkle, without a sin. It is to be put back beyond Eden. God looks over His ledger, and says:

"Moody, I have no account against you. Your debt has all been wiped out by another."

November 21st.

But if the Spirit of Him that raised up Jesus from the dead dwell in you, He that raised up Christ from the dead shall also quicken your mortal bodies by His Spirit that dwelleth in you.—Romans viii. 11.

I HAD rather be in the heart of the eighth of Romans than Adam in the heart of Paradise. Adam might have stayed in Paradise ten thousand years, and the devil could have come in then and snatched his life away from him, but I challenge the devil himself to get my life away from me, because it is hid with Christ in God, and Christ conquered Satan. "The prince of this world cometh, and hath nothing in Me." Christ conquered him, and oh, how safe the believer is! When the sinner is hid in Christ, hid in God, how is Satan going to get at him? He must go by the Almighty and by Christ before he can get at that sinner.

It is a great thing to be an heir of glory. It is a great thing to have your life guarded by the Son of God, and to have the angels of God encamping round about you.

November 22d.

And when they came to Jesus, they besought Him instantly, saying, That he was worthy for whom He should do this: for he loveth our nation, and he hath built us a synagogue.—Luke vii. 4, 5.

THE Jews could not understand grace, so they thought Christ would grant the request of this man, because he was worthy.

"Why," they said, "he hath built us a syna-gogue!"

It is the same old story that we hear to-day. Let a man give a few thousand dollars to build a church and he must have the best pew; "he is worthy." Perhaps he made his money by sell-ing or making strong drink; but he has put the church under an obligation by this gift of money, and he is considered "worthy." This same spirit was at work in the days of Christ.

NOVEMBER 23d.

Be sure your sin will find you out.—Numbers xxxii. 23.

DO you want to know the reason why, every now and then, the church is scandalized by the exposure of some leading church member or Sabbath-school superintendent? It is not his Christianity, but his lack of it. Some secret sin has been eating at the heart of the tree, and in a critical moment it is blown down and its rotten-ness revealed.

NOVEMBER 24th.

Give ear, O My people, to My law : incline your ears to the words of My mouth.—Psalm lxxviii. 1.

MAN lost spiritual life and communion with his Maker by listening to the voice of the tempter, instead of the voice of God. We get life again by listening to the voice of God. The Word of God gives life. "The words that I speak unto you," says Christ, "they are spirit, and they are life." So, what people need is—to incline their ear, and HEAR.

It is a great thing when the preacher gets the ear of a congregation—I mean the inner ear, for a man has not only two ears in his head; he has what we may call the outer ear and the inner ear—the ear of the soul. You may speak to the outward ear, and not reach the ear of the soul at all. Many in these days are like the "foolish people" to whom the prophet Jeremiah spoke: "Which have eyes, and see not; which have ears, and hear not." "He that hath ears to hear, let him hear."

NOVEMBER 25th.

And Nathanael said unto him, Can there any good thing come out of Nazareth? Philip saith unto him, Come and see.—John i. 46.

SO we say to you, "Come and see!" I thought, when I was converted, that my friends had been very unfaithful to me, because they had not told me about Christ. I thought I would have all my friends converted inside of twenty-four hours, and I was quite disappointed when they did not at once see Christ to be the Lily of the Valley, and the Rose of Sharon, and the Bright and Morning Star. I wondered why it was. But we need to learn that God alone can do that.

November 26th.

If ye were of the world, the world would love his own: but because ye are not of the world, but I have chosen you out of the world, therefore the world hateth you. Remember the word that I said unto you, The servant is not greater than his lord. If they have persecuted Me, they will also persecute you; if they have kept My saying, they will keep yours also.—John xv. 19, 20.

NOW mark you, no man can be true for God, and live for Him, without at some time or other being unpopular in this world. Those men who are trying to live for both worlds make a wreck of it; for at some time or other the collision is sure to come.

November 27th.

And I said unto the king, if it please the king, and if Thy servant have found favor in Thy sight, that thou wouldest send me unto Jndah, unto the city of my fathers' sepulchres, that I may build it.—Nehemiah ii. 5.

IT meant a good deal for Nehemiah to give up the palace of Shushan and his high office, and identify himself with the despised and captive Jews. He was among the highest in the whole realm. Not only that, but he was a man of wealth, lived in ease and luxury, and had great influence at court. For him to go to Jerusalem and lose caste was like Moses turning his back on the palace of Pharaoh and identifying himself with the Hebrew slaves. Yet we might never have heard of either of them if they had not done this. They stooped to conquer; and when you get ready to stoop God will bless you. Plato, Socrates, and other Greek philosophers lived in the same century as Nehemiah. How few have heard of them and read their words compared with the hundreds of thousands who have heard and read of Nehemiah during the last two thousand years!

November 28th.

They that will be (that is, desire to be) rich fall into temptation and a snare, and into many foolish and hurtful lusts, which drown men in destruction and perdition.—1 Timothy vi. 9.

THE Bible speaks of the deceitfulness of two things—"the deceitfulness of *sin*" and "the deceitfulness of *riches*." Riches are like a mirage in the desert, which has all the appearance of satisfying, and lures on the traveller with the promise of water and shade; but he only wastes his strength in the effort to reach it. So riches never satisfy: the pursuit of them always turns out a snare.

November 29th.

There was also a strife among them, which of them should be accounted the greatest.—Luke xxii. 24.

TO me, one of the saddest things in all the life of Jesus Christ was the fact that just before His crucifixion, His disciples should have been striving to see who should be the greatest. It was His last night on earth, and they never saw Him so sorrowful before. He knew Judas was going to sell Him for thirty pieces of silver. He knew that Peter would deny Him. And yet, in addition to this, when going into the very shadow of the cross, there arose this strife as to who should be the greatest.

He took a towel and girded Himself like a slave, and He took a basin of water and stooped and washed their feet. That was another object lesson of humility. He said, "Ye call Me Master and Lord, and ye say well." If you want to be great in My Kingdom, be servant of all. If you serve, you shall be great.

November 30th.

Your heart shall rejoice, and your joy no man taketh from you.—John xvi. 22.

I AM so thankful that I have a joy that the world cannot rob me of; I have a treasure that the world cannot take from me; I have something that it is not in the power of man or devil to deprive me of, the joy of the Lord. "No man taketh it from you."

DECEMBER 1st.

And Lot went out, and spake unto his sons-in-law, which married his daughters, and said, Up, get you out of this place; for the Lord will destroy this city. But he seemed as one that mocked unto his sons-in-law.— Genesis xix. 14.

THE Saviour tells us they were eating and drinking, buying and selling, planting and building; all went on as usual. Sodom was never more prosperous than now. There is no sign of a coming judgment; no sign that Sodom is going to be burnt up.

The sun shone as brightly the day before its destruction as it had shone for years. The stars perhaps were glittering in the heavens as brightly as ever, and the moon threw her light down upon the city; but Lot's sons-in-law mocked him, he couldn't get them out. I see him going through the streets with his head bowed down, and great tears trickling down his cheeks. Ask him now about his life, and he will tell you it has been a total failure. He goes back to his home; and early in the morning the angels have to take him almost by force, and hasten him out of the city. He could not bear the thought of leaving his loved ones there to perish, while God dealt in judgment with that city.

Is not that a fair picture of hundreds and thousands at the present time? Have you been trying to accumulate wealth even to the neglect of your children, so that to-day they are lifting

up their voices against your God, and against
your Bible, and against you? They do not
care for your feelings; are they not trampling
them under their feet? Perhaps many of the
parents have gone to their graves, and the children are now squandering what their parents
gathered. What an example we have in the
case of Lot, and how it ought to open the eyes
of many a business man, and cause him to see
that his life is going to be a total wreck if he
takes his children into Sodom's judgment when
the judgment comes.

DECEMBER 2d.

*For I delivered unto you first of all that which I also
received, how that Christ died for our sins according to
the scriptures.*—1 Corinthians xv. 3.

YOU ask me what my hope is. It is that
Christ died for my sins, in my stead, in
my place, and therefore I can enter into life
eternal. You ask Paul what his hope was.
"Christ died for our sins according to the
Scripture." This is the hope in which died all
the glorious martyrs of old, in which all who
have entered heaven's gate have found their
only comfort. Take that doctrine of substitu-
tion out of the Bible, and my hope is lost.
With the law, without Christ, we are all un-
done. The law we have broken, and it can
only hang over our head the sharp sword of
justice. Even if we could keep it from this

moment, there remains the unforgiven past. "Without shedding of blood there is no remission."

DECEMBER 3d.

Now Naaman, captain of the host of the king of Syria, was a great man with his master, and honorable, because by him the Lord had given deliverance unto Syria: he was also a mighty man in valor, but he was a leper.—2 Kings v. 1.

DID you ever ask yourselves which is the worse—the leprosy of sin, or the leprosy of the body? For my own part, I would a thousand times sooner have the leprosy of the body eating into my eyes, and feet, and arms! I would rather be loathsome in the sight of my fellow-men than die with the leprosy of sin in my soul, and be banished from God forever! The leprosy of the body is bad, but the leprosy of sin is a thousand times worse. It has cast angels out of heaven. It has ruined the best and strongest men that ever lived in the world. Oh, how it has pulled men down!

DECEMBER 4th.

And the Spirit and the bride say, Come. And let him that heareth say, Come. And let him that is athirst come. And whosoever will, let him take the water of life freely.—Revelation xxii. 17.

HOW many men fold their arms and say: "If I am one of the elect, I will be saved, and if I am not, I won't. No use bothering about it."

I have an idea that the Lord Jesus saw how men were going to stumble over this doctrine of election, so after He had been thirty or forty years in heaven He came down and spoke to John. One Lord's day in Patmos, He said to him:

"Write these things to the churches."

John kept on writing. His pen flew very fast. And then the Lord, when it was nearly finished, said,

"John, before you close the book, put in one more invitation. 'The Spirit and the bride say, Come. And let him that heareth say, Come. And let him that is athirst, come. And WHOSOEVER WILL, let him take the water of life freely.'"

DECEMBER 5th.

The wages of sin is death; but the gift of God is eternal life through Jesus Christ our Lord.—Romans vi. 23.

IF an angel came straight from the throne of God, and proclaimed that God has sent him to offer us any one thing we might ask—that each one should have his own petition granted— what would be your cry? There would be but one response, and the cry would make heaven ring: "Eternal life! eternal life!" Everything else would float away into nothingness.

It is life men want, and value most. Let a

man worth a million dollars be on a wrecked
vessel, and if he could save his life for six
months by giving that million, he would give it
in an instant. But the gospel is a six months'
gift; " *The gift of God is eternal life.*" And is
it not one of the greatest marvels that men have
to stand and plead and pray and beseech their
fellow-men to take this precious gift of God?

DECEMBER 6th.

*Know ye not that your body is the temple of the Holy
Ghost which is in you, which ye have of God, and ye
are not your own? for ye are bought with a price:
therefore glorify God in your body and in your spirit,
which are God's.*—1 Corinthians vi. 19, 20.

I THINK it is clearly taught in the Scripture
that every believer has the Holy Ghost
dwelling in him, that there is a divine resident
in every child of God. He may be quenching
the Spirit of God, and he may not glorify God
as he should, but if he is a believer on the Lord
Jesus Christ, the Holy Ghost dwells in him.
But I want to call attention to another fact. I
believe to-day that though Christian men and
women have the Holy Spirit dwelling in them,
He is not dwelling within them in power; in
other words, God has a great many sons and
daughters without power.

December 7th.

And I was afraid, and went and hid thy talent in the earth: lo, there thou hast that is thine.—Matthew xxv. 25.

I READ of a man who had a thousand dollars. He hid it away, thinking he would in that way take care of it, and that when he was an old man he would have something to fall back upon. After keeping the deposit receipt for twenty years he took it to a bank and got just one thousand dollars for it. If he had put the money at interest in the usual way, he might have had three times the amount.

He made the mistake that a great many people are making to-day throughout Christendom, of not trading with his talents. My experience has been as I have gone about in the world and mingled with professing Christians, that those who find most fault with others are those who themselves do nothing. If a person is busy improving the talents that God has given him he will have too much to do to find fault and complain about others.

December 8th.

I know Whom I have believed, and am persuaded that He is able to keep that which I have committed unto Him against that day.—2 Timothy i. 12.

NOTICE the confidence that breathes through Paul's last words to Timothy. It is not a matter of doubt, but of knowledge: "I know," "I am persuaded."

The word " Hope " is not used in the Scripture to express doubt. It is used in regard to the second coming of Christ, or to the resurrection of the body. We should not say that we " hope " we are Christians. I do not say that I " hope " I am an American, or that I " hope " I am a married man. These are settled things. I may say that I " hope " to go back to my home, or that I hope to attend such a meeting. If we are born of God we know it; He will not leave us in darkness if we search the Scriptures.

December 9th.

Greater love hath no man than this, that a man lay down his life for his friends.—John xv. 13.

WHEN we wish to know the love of God we should go to Calvary. Can we look upon that scene, and say God did not love us? That cross speaks of the love of God. Greater love never has been taught than that which the cross teaches. What prompted God to give up Christ—what prompted Christ to die—if it were not love? " Greater love hath no man than this, that a man lay down his life for his friends." Christ laid down His life for His enemies; Christ laid down His life for His murderers; Christ laid down His life for them that hated Him; and the spirit of the cross, the spirit of Calvary, is love. When they were mocking Him and deriding Him, what did He say? "Father, forgive them, for they know not what they do." That is love. He did not call down fire from heaven to consume them; there was nothing but love in His heart.

DECEMBER 10th.

Jesus saith unto him, I am the way, the truth, and the life: no man cometh unto the Father, but by Me. —John xiv. 6.

PEOPLE say: "I want to know what is the truth."

Listen: "I AM THE TRUTH," says Christ. (John xiv. 5.) If you want to know what the truth is, get acquainted with Christ.

People also complain that they have not life. Many are trying to give themselves spiritual life. You may galvanize yourselves and put electricity into yourselves, so to speak; but the effect will not last very long. Christ alone is the author of life. If you would have real spiritual life, get to know Christ. Many try to stir up spiritual life by going to meetings. These may be well enough; but it will be of no use, unless they get into contact with the living Christ. Then spiritual life will not be a spasmodic thing, but will be perpetual; flowing on and on, and bringing forth fruit to God.

DECEMBER 11th.

As we have borne the image of the earthly, we shall also bear the image of the heavenly.—1 Corinthians xv. 49.

THANK God, we are to gain by death! We are to have something that death cannot touch. When this earthly body is raised, all the present imperfection will be gone. Jacob will leave his lameness. Paul will have no thorn in the flesh. We shall enter a life that deserves the name of life, happy, glorious, everlasting—the body once more united to the soul, no longer mortal, subject to pain and disease and death, but glorified, incorruptible, " fashioned like unto His glorious body," everything that hinders the spiritual life left behind. We are exiles now, but then we who are faithful shall stand before the throne of God, joint heirs with Christ, kings and priests, citizens of that heavenly country.

DECEMBER 12th.

We know that all things work together for good to them that love God, to them that are called according to His purpose.—Romans viii. 28.

I HAVE an idea we will thank God in eternity for our reverses and trials more than for anything else. I believe John Bunyan thanked God for the Bedford Jail more than for anything that happened to him down here. I believe Paul thanked God for the rods and stripes more than for anything else that happened to him.

Are you passing through the waters? Don't get discouraged! You are an heir of glory; He is with you. He was with Joseph when he was cast into prison. I had rather be in prison with the Almighty than outside without Him. You needn't be afraid of prison, and, you needn't be afraid of the grave, you needn't be afraid of death. Cheer up, child of God; the time of our redemption draweth near! We may have to suffer a little while, but when you think of the eternal weight of glory, you can afford to suffer.

DECEMBER 13th.

O the depth of the riches both of the wisdom and knowledge of God! how unsearchable are His judgments, and His ways past finding out!—Romans xi. 33.

I THANK God there is a height in the Bible I do not know anything about, a depth I have never been able to fathom, and it makes the Book all the more fascinating. If I could take that Book up and read it as I can any other book and understand it at one reading, I should have lost faith in it years ago. It is one of the strongest proofs that it must have come from God, that the acutest men who have dug for fifty years have laid down their pens and said,

" There is a depth we know nothing of." " No Scripture," said Spurgeon, " is exhausted by a single explanation. The flowers of God's garden bloom, not only double, but sevenfold: they are continually pouring forth fresh fragrance."

DECEMBER 14th.

Christ hath redeemed us from the curse of the law, being made a curse for us : for it is written, Cursed is every one that hangeth on a tree.—Galatians iii. 13.

LIFE never came through the law. As some one has observed : " When the law was given, three thousand men lost life; but when grace and truth came at Pentecost, three thousand obtained life." Under the law, if a man became a drunkard the magistrates would take him out and stone him to death. When the prodigal came home, grace met him and embraced him. Law said, Stone him !—grace said, Embrace him ! Law said, Smite him !—grace said, Kiss him ! Law went after him, and bound him; grace said, Loose him and let him go ! Law tells me how crooked I am; grace comes and makes me straight.

DECEMBER 15th.

Therefore his sisters sent unto him, saying, Lord, behold, he whom Thou lovest is sick.—John xi. 3.

THE communion those sisters had with Jesus brought them so near to His heart that when the time of trouble came they knew where to go for comfort. A great many people do not learn that secret in prosperity, and so when the billows come rolling up against them, they don't know which way to turn. The darkest and most wretched place on the face of the earth, is a home where death has entered, and where Christ is unknown. No hope of a resurrection, no hope of a brighter day coming.

December 16th.

Now when Daniel knew that the writing was signed, he went into his house; and his windows being open in his chamber toward Jerusalem, he kneeled upon his knees three times a day, and prayed, and gave thanks before his God, as he did aforetime.—Daniel vi. 10.

THERE is many a business man to-day who will tell you he has no time to pray: his business is so pressing that he cannot call his family around him, and ask God to bless them. He is so busy that he cannot ask God to keep him and them from the temptations of the present life—the temptations of every day. "Business is so pressing." I am reminded of the words of an old Methodist minister: "If you have so much business to attend to that you have no time to pray, depend upon it you have more business on hand than God ever intended you should have."

But look at this man. He had the whole, or nearly the whole, of the king's business to attend to. He was Prime Minister, Secretary of State, and Secretary of the Treasury, all in one. He had to attend to all his own work, and to give an eye to the work of lots of other men. And yet he found time to pray : not just now and then, nor once in a way, not just when he happened to have a few moments to spare, but " three times a day."

DECEMBER 17th,

They have sown the wind, and they shall reap the whirlwind.—Hosea viii. 7.

WHENEVER I hear a young man talking in a flippant way about sowing his wild oats, I don't laugh. I feel more like crying, because I know he is going to make his grey-haired mother reap in tears ; he is going to make his wife reap in shame ; he is going to make his old father and his innocent children reap with him. Only ten or fifteen or twenty years will pass before he will have to reap his wild oats ; no man has ever sowed them without having to reap them. Sow the wind and you reap the whirlwind.

December 18th.

That Christ may dwell in your hearts by faith; that ye, being rooted and grounded in love, may be able to comprehend with all saints what is the breadth, and length, and depth, and height; and to know the love of Christ, which passeth knowledge, that ye might be filled with all the fullness of God.—Ephesians iii. 17–19.

MANY of us think we know something of God's love, but centuries hence we shall admit we have never found out much about it. Columbus discovered America; but what did he know about its great lakes, rivers, forests, and the Mississippi valley? He died, without knowing much about what he had discovered. So, many of us have discovered something of the love of God, but there are heights, depths and lengths of it we do not know. That Love is a great ocean, and we require to plunge into it before we really know anything of it.

Among the many victims of the Paris Commune was a Catholic bishop. He was a man who knew something of the love of God in his own experience. In the little cell where he was confined, awaiting execution, was a small window in the shape of a cross. After his death there was found written above the cross "height"; below it, "depth"; and at the end of each arm of the cross, "length" and "breadth." He had learned that God's love was unfailing in the hour of adversity and death.

December 19th.

If any of you lack wisdom, let him ask of God, that giveth to all men liberally, and upbraideth not; and it shall be given him. But let him ask in faith, nothing wavering. For he that wavereth is like a wave of the sea driven with the wind and tossed.—James i. 5, 6.

SO faith is the golden key that unlocks the treasures of heaven. It was the shield that David took when he met Goliath on the field; he believed that God was going to deliver the Philistine into his hands. Some one has said that faith could lead Christ about anywhere; wherever He found it He honored it.

Unbelief sees something in God's hand, and says, " I cannot get it." Faith sees it, and says, " I will have it."

December 20th.

Having loved His own that were in the world, He loved them unto the end.—John xiii. 1.

IT is recorded of Jesus Christ, just when He was about to be departed from His disciples and led away to Calvary, that: " having loved His own which were in the world, He loved them unto the end." He knew that one of His disciples would betray Him, yet He loved Judas. He knew that another disciple would deny Him, and swear that he never knew Him, and yet He loved Peter. It was the love which Christ had for Peter that broke his heart, and brought him back in penitence to the feet of his Lord. For three years Jesus had been with the disciples trying to teach them His love, not only by His life and words, but by His works. And on the night of His betrayal He takes a basin of water, girds Himself with a towel, and taking the place of a servant, washes their feet; He wants to convince them of His unchanging love.

DECEMBER 21st.

I will honor Him.—Psalm xci. 15.

GOD'S honor is something worth seeking. Man's honor doesn't amount to much. Suppose Moses had stopped down there in Egypt. He would have been loaded down with Egyptian titles, but they would never have reached us. Suppose he had been Chief Marshal of the whole Egyptian army, "General" Moses, "Commander" Moses; suppose he had reached the throne and become one of those Pharaohs, and his mummy had come down to our day. What is that compared with the honor God put upon him? How his name shines on the page of history!

The honor of this world doesn't last, it is transient, it passes away; and I don't believe any man or woman is fit for God's service that is looking for worldly preferment, worldly honors and worldly fame. Let us get it under our feet, let us rise above it, and seek the honor that comes down from above.

December 22d.

(Mr. Moody's " Coronation Day.")

Verily, verily, I say unto you, If a man keep My saying, he shall never see death.—John viii. 51.

SOME day you will read in the papers that D. L. Moody, of East Northfield, is dead. Don't you believe a word of it! At that moment I shall be more alive than I am now. I shall have gone up higher, that is all; gone out of this old clay tenement into a house that is immortal, a body that death cannot touch, that sin cannot taint, a body like unto His own glorious body. I was born of the flesh in 1837. I was born of the Spirit in 1856. That which is born of the flesh may die. That which is born of the Spirit will live forever.

December 23d.

Verily, verily, I say unto you, he that heareth My word and believeth on Him that sent Me, hath everlasting life, and shall not come into condemnation ; but is passed from death unto life.—John v. 24.

SALVATION is instantaneous. I admit that a man may be converted so that he cannot tell when he crossed the line between death and life, but I also believe a man may be a thief one moment and a saint the next. I believe a man may be as vile as hell itself one moment, and be saved the next.

Christian growth is gradual, just as physical growth is; but a man passes from death unto everlasting life quick as an act of the will— "He that believeth on the Son *hath* everlasting life."

DECEMBER 24th.

And God shall wipe away all tears from their eyes: and there shall be no more death, neither sorrow, nor crying, neither shall there be any more pain: for the former things are passed away.—Revelation xxi. 4.

THERE are no tears in heaven, and there would be few on earth if the will of God was only done.

DECEMBER 25th.

And she brought forth her firstborn Son, and wrapped Him in swaddling clothes, and laid Him in a manger; because there was no room for them in the inn.—Luke ii. 7.

THE natural human heart is like that inn at Bethlehem—no room for Christ! Every true saint of God for four thousand years had been gazing out into the future, looking and listening that they might hear the footfall of the Coming One. Bible students think that when Eve brought forth her firstborn and said: "I have got a man from the Lord," she thought he was the Promised One. And right on for four thousand years the mothers in Israel had been looking for that Child. And now the time has arrived. He appears on earth; and the first thing we read is that there is no room for Him!

He came on no secret mission. He tells us what He came for, "to seek and to save that which was lost." He came to get His arm under the vilest sinner and lift him up to God; to bind up the broken-hearted, and to comfort those that mourn. And yet from time to time it was announced in Jerusalem that He had come, until He was put to death on the cross, the sword was not put back into its scabbard until it had pierced the very heart of the God-man.

DECEMBER 26th.

(*Mr. Moody's Burial.*)

So when this corruptible shall have put on incorruption, and this mortal shall have put on immortality, then shall be brought to pass the saying that is written, Death is swallowed up in victory. O death, where is thy sting? O grave, where is thy victory?—I Corinthians xv. 54, 55.

I TURN my back on death, and journey toward life from this time on, and away into the eternity beyond the grave I see LIFE.

DECEMBER 27th.

Honor thy father and thy mother: that thy days may be long upon the land which the Lord thy God giveth thee.—Exodus xx. 12.

THE one glimpse the Bible gives us of thirty out of the thirty-three years of Christ's life on earth shows that He did not come to destroy the fifth commandment. The secret of all those silent years is embodied in that verse in Luke's Gospel—"And He went down with them and came also to Nazareth, and was subject to them." Did He not set an example of true filial love and care when in the midst of the agonies of the cross He made provision for His mother?

DECEMBER 28th.

And I beheld, and I heard the voice of many angels round about the throne and the beasts and the elders: and the number of them was ten thousand times ten thousand, and thousands of thousands; saying with a loud voice, Worthy is the Lamb that was slain to receive power, and riches, and wisdom, and strength, and honor, and glory, and blessing.—Revelation v. 11, 12.

YES, He is worthy of all this. Heaven cannot speak too well of Him. Oh that earth would take up the echo, and join with heaven in singing, "WORTHY to receive power, and riches, and wisdom, and strength, and honor, and glory, and blessing!"

December 29th.

As far as the east is from the west, so far hath He removed our transgressions from us.—Psalm ciii. 12.

NOT *some* of them; He takes them *all* away. You may pile up your sins till they rise like a dark mountain, and then multiply them by ten thousand for those you cannot think of; and after you have tried to enumerate all the sins you have ever committed, just let me bring one verse in, and that mountain will melt away: " The blood of Jesus Christ, His Son, cleanseth us from ALL sin."

December 30th.

And the Lord God called unto Adam, and said unto him, Where art thou?—Genesis iii. 9.

A MAN once said to me, " How do you know that God put that question to Adam?"
The best answer I can give is, Because He has put it to me many a time. I doubt whether there ever has been a son or a daughter of Adam who has not heard that voice ringing through the soul many a time. Who am I? What am I? Where am I going? So let us put the question to ourselves personally, Where am I? Not in the sight of man—that is of very little account; but where am I in the sight of God?

DECEMBER 31st.

With long life will I satisfy him.—Psalm xci. 16.

I GET a good deal of comfort out of that promise. I don't think that means a short life down here, seventy years, eighty years, ninety years, or one hundred years. Do you think that any man living would be satisfied if they could live to be one hundred years old and then have to die? Not by a good deal. Suppose Adam had lived until to-day and had to die to-night, would he be satisfied? Not a bit of it! Not if he had lived a million years, and then had to die.

You know we are all the time coming to the end of things here,—the end of the week, the end of the month, the end of the year, the end of school days. It is end, end, end all the time. But, thank God, He is going to satisfy us with long life; no end to it, an endless life.

Life is very sweet. I never liked death; I like life. It would be a pretty dark world if death was eternal, and when our loved ones die we are to be eternally separated from them. Thank God, it is not so; we shall be reunited. It is just moving out of this house into a better one; stepping up higher, and living on and on forever.

Other titles by/on D L Moody

An Inspirational Treasury of D L Moody (by Stanley Barnes)
D L Moody - Soul Winner (by Chester Mann)
Prevailing Prayer (by D L Moody)

Other Devotionals from Ambassador

If you enjoyed reading From Day to Day try some of these!

A Text A Day (by Dr. Ian R K Paisley)
Daily Light - KJV (by Samuel Bagster)
Diary of a Longing Heart (by Derick Bingham)
Eagles' Wings (Edited by Alan Cairns)
For All Seasons (by Derick Bingham)
God Makes A Path (by Robert Murray McCheyne)
God's Treasury (by C. H. Spurgeon)
Into The Millennium (by Dr. Ian R K Paisley)
The Invitation - John's Gospel (by Derick Bingham)
The Long Road Home - Ezra & Nehemiah (by Samuel T. Carson)
My Power Diary (for children) - (by Rhonda Paisley)
On Highest Ground - Ephesians (by Derick Bingham)
*The Ambassador Treasury of Daily Devotions - (Compiled from the
writings of Murray, Muller, Booth, Torrey, Bounds, Wesley, Ryle,
Havergal, Spurgeon and many more!)*
Waiting on God (by Andrew Murray)
Quiet Time (by George B Duncan)